Subtle Wisdom

Doubleday
New York   London   Toronto
Sydney   Auckland

Subtle Wisdom

Understanding

Suffering,

Cultivating

Compassion

Through

Ch'an

Buddhism

Master Sheng-yen

PUBLISHED BY DOUBLEDAY
a division of Random House, Inc.

DOUBLEDAY and the portrayal of an anchor
with a dolphin are trademarks of Doubleday,
a division of Random House, Inc.

Book design by Jennifer Ann Daddio
Calligraphy by Nora Ling-yun Shih

Library of Congress Cataloging-in-Publication Data

Sheng-yen.
Subtle wisdom: understanding suffering, cultivating
compassion through Ch'an buddhism /
Master Sheng-yen.
p.   cm.
1. Zen Buddhism.   2. Suffering—Religious
aspects—Buddhism.   3. Compassion (Buddhism)
I. Title.
BQ9265.4.S477   1999
294.3'927—dc21   99-21089
CIP

ISBN 0-385-48045-8
Copyright © 1999 by Dharma Drum Publications

All Rights Reserved
Printed in the United States of America
September 1999
First Edition

1   3   5   7   9   10   8   6   4   2

Thus shall ye think of this fleeting world:
A star at dawn, a bubble in a stream;
A flash of lightning in a summer cloud,
A flickering lamp, a phantom and a dream.

—*The Diamond Sutra*

Contents

Introduction

I would like to take this opportunity to describe the background and development of Ch'an, both for readers who are new to Ch'an and for those who have little or erroneous information.

Ch'an cannot be separated from Buddhism. Since the time of Buddha, masters have given "transmission" of his wisdom to their disciples when they demonstrated experience and understanding of the Dharma, the teachings of Buddha. As a result of this form of recognition, lineages have developed and have become separate sects or schools of Buddhism. This does not mean that each sect holds only part of the Buddhadharma. What is transmitted in the Ch'an school is, in fact, the whole of the Dharma.

The Dharma is like the ocean. Whether you take water from the Indian Ocean, the Atlantic Ocean, or the Arctic Ocean, it always tastes salty. Likewise, in all the lineages within mainstream Buddhism, the taste of Dharma is the same. The taste is the whole of Shakyamuni Buddha's teaching.

Who was Shakyamuni, the founder of Buddhism? Shakyamuni Buddha is not a mythical figure; he was born over twenty-six hundred years ago, the prince of the small kingdom of the Shakya clan in what is now Nepal.

At a certain point Prince Shakyamuni was confronted with the inevitability of old age, sickness, and death, and he asked himself why these are inherent parts of the human condition. He was gravely concerned with this question, and his inability to solve it led him to leave his household and become a spiritual seeker in the traditional Indian way. If you know a bit about Indian history and religion you know that the Indian subcontinent has a rich history of spiritual practice, and a supportive atmosphere for such practice. Shakyamuni hoped to realize enlightenment, and through his enlightenment to resolve the questions about the reasons for birth, sickness, old age, and death.

For the next six years Shakyamuni mainly cultivated two kinds of practice. The first was *samadhi*, the practice of meditative concentration and absorption. The second was asceticism. Neither of these resolved his questions about our basic human condition. Even though he was able to reach profound states of mind, he was not enlightened.

After six years of practicing *samadhi* and asceticism, he gave them up. He felt that asceticism, in particular, was not in accordance with wisdom, and later advocated the "Middle Way."[1] Shakyamuni continued to meditate, and one day as he was coming out of meditation quite naturally, with a relaxed and joyful mind, he looked up at the sky and saw the morning star, and his perception was transformed. He realized that originally, intrinsically, the mind is unlimited. All things are just as they are. There is no need to give rise to vexations.[2] At that moment he was completely enlightened.

Buddhism teaches that although all things are spontaneously, naturally, just as they are, without afflictions and vexations, sentient beings have been unaware of this since time without beginning; that is, their mind ground[3] is not luminous and bright. Because of this unawareness, living beings cherish themselves and concern themselves greatly with what they experience and especially with what they like and dislike and whether they gain or lose. Even when we gain something we suffer because we fear losing it. We hold on to objects, experiences, and feelings with

---

1. The Middle Way teaches avoidance of all extremes as part of the way that leads to release from suffering. This means avoiding indulgence in the pleasures of the senses, on one hand, and self-mortification and asceticism on the other.
2. Vexations (Sanskrit: *Klesa*) are attitudes, views, emotional states, and other conditions arising from attachment, which cause suffering or disharmony.
3. "Mind ground" refers to the intrinsic nature of the mind, and thus to Buddha nature.

great attachment. Out of this attachment we create separateness between ourselves and our environment, and all phenomena. We alienate ourselves into individual "I's." Because of this illusory separateness and our attachment to the individual "I," we go through cycles of birth, sickness, aging, and death; and suffering is the result of this process.

The Buddhist view is that the experience of the individual "I," the clinging to "I," even the understanding and experience of inseparability of the self and the environment, are all impermanent. What we experience as self and environment are temporary and constantly changing, and if we are attached to them they cause us suffering. Through letting go of all attachments and giving rise to wisdom—the realization of impermanence—our minds can regain their luminosity and become enlightened.

What Shakyamuni Buddha realized is summarized in the "Four Noble Truths" of Buddhism, one of his earliest teachings: 1) suffering, 2) the cause of suffering, 3) the cessation of suffering, and 4) the path that leads to the extinction of suffering.

Suffering is unawareness of the impermanent nature of all things. Because of this we create illusions, we project, we attach to ourselves and to other phenomena, and we create suffering.

Because of our misunderstanding of the nature of phenomena, we find ourselves in constant struggle, rejecting what we dislike and seeking what we desire. This rejecting and seeking is the *cause of suffering*.

Buddha taught *the cessation of suffering*. He wanted us to realize that on one hand, suffering can be overcome; and that on the other hand, even suffering is impermanent. If we can engage in practice and personally realize the fleeting nature of all things, then suffering will be extinguished. The way to do this is by following *the path*, the Eightfold Path of Buddhism, which involves eight particular activities.[4] The extinguishing of suffering was what Shakyamuni realized himself, and what he wanted others to realize.

How do the Four Noble Truths of Buddha's teaching and realization relate to Ch'an Buddhism? While Ch'an does not explicitly talk about and explain the Four Noble Truths, nevertheless it retains their spirit.

In the Ch'an school we talk about no mind, no form, no abiding, and no thought. These four "no's," which are more commonly known in the west as the idea of "no self," refer to the substancelessness of the self. The four "no's" are the result of letting go of one's clinging attachment to the sense of "I," and to the illusion of the permanence of the self and phenomena. When you can understand and realize the workings of impermanence and the reality of no self, you have realized no mind, no form, no abiding, and no thought, as well as the Four Noble Truths.

In Ch'an practice we try to incorporate the Four Noble Truths into all aspects of daily life. We apply them dynamically, so that the practice becomes inseparable from daily life. In this way we overcome the tendency to see spiritual practice as something special, separate from ordinary situations and challenges.

---

4. The Eightfold Path: 1) Right Understanding. 2) Right Thought. 3) Right Speech. 4) Right Action. 5) Right Livelihood. 6) Right Effort. 7) Right Mindfulness. 8) Right Concentration.

How did Ch'an Buddhism develop in China after Indian Buddhism was introduced into China? From the perspective of the Ch'an tradition itself—according to its mythology—Shakyamuni Buddha transmitted the Dharma to Mahakashyapa, the first "patriarch" of Ch'an (meaning that he recognized Mahakashyapa's realization of enlightenment). Mahakashyapa transmitted to Ananda the Honored One, and so on from generation to generation, for twenty-six generations in India. Thus a lineage of awakened, enlightened minds was created, each recognized by the previous patriarch. The twenty-eighth Indian Patriarch was Bodhidharma (believed to have lived about 470–543), who went to China and became the first patriarch there, beginning the Chinese Ch'an lineage.

What exactly did Bodhidharma take to China? All he took with him, what he wanted to share with the Chinese people, was the knowledge that Buddhadharma is present everywhere and is constantly manifesting itself. Because of beginningless ignorance, living beings are unable to recognize the Buddhadharma, so Bodhidharma also pointed out ways to fully realize that the Buddhadharma is everywhere. By the time of the sixth Chinese Ch'an Patriarch, Huineng (in Japanese, *E'no*, 638–713), the ideas and principles of Indian Ch'an Buddhism had been assimilated into, and altered by, the Chinese mind and culture. Fully Chinese forms had developed, and Ch'an began to be widely accepted and propagated.

Shakyamuni himself was cultured and intelligent; however, his disciples were people of all levels of intellectual capacity and came from all segments of society. There were some who were extremely intelligent and others who were not. There were learned people and ignorant people. Yet all of them were able to awaken to the path that leads to enlightenment. This is because the realization of the Buddha's teaching is not an intellectual or philosophical pursuit. Buddhadharma places great importance on personally actualizing the teaching so that it can be put into practice in daily life. Only in this way can the Buddhadharma free us from the fetters of disturbing emotional afflictions and suffering, and enable us to realize enlightenment. Master Huineng was himself a firewood cutter with no education. However, after his enlightenment his teaching and actions were spontaneously in perfect accordance with the Buddha's teaching. We should always remember that the Dharma is not exclusively for people with keen intelligence. It is for everyone. Anyone who is interested in the Dharma and works hard can reach enlightenment.

A distinctive characteristic of Ch'an is that although we place emphasis on sitting meditation, we do not believe that sitting meditation can produce enlightenment. In the records of the life and teaching of Huineng we don't see any mention of him engaging in sitting meditation. The same is true of his immediate spiritual descendants.

There is a story that illustrates the deluded nature of believing that sitting meditation produces enlightenment. A master asked a *bhiksu* (a fully ordained monk) who was sitting in meditation what he was doing. The *bhiksu* said he was trying to become a Buddha. The master said that was like polishing a brick hoping to make a mirror. Rubbing a brick does not produce mirrors. Likewise, sitting meditation does not produce Buddhas.

This is in accordance with Shakyamuni Buddha's example. Shakyamuni himself gave up ascetic practice and mere meditative absorption practice before he became enlightened. The Ch'an tradition follows the example of Shakyamuni Buddha in spirit.

To return to the history of the lineage of Ch'an: in the seventh generation in China, the lineage split into two sub-lineages. Later these two sub-lineages split into five and then seven lineages. Only two of these have survived to the present, Linji and Caodong. The modern Linji tradition is not really in the direct line of Master Linji, but in the line of a sub-school which has continued since Linji. I, myself, am a lineage holder in both of these two existing schools, Linji and Caodong.

Chinese masters transmitted Ch'an to Japan and Korea. In Japan both the Linji and the Caodong traditions were transmitted and became the Rinzai and Soto schools of Zen. Since then Zen has gone through many transformations and changes in Japan. About thirty different Rinzai sub-schools have developed. This is partly because different Chinese masters transmitted Ch'an to Japan at different times. However, those transmission lineages also subdivided in Japan. In Soto Zen the lineage mainly comes from the Chinese Caodong master, Hongzhi Zhenjue, of Mt. Tiantong in China. Although I am a recipient of Caodong transmission, it is a different lineage from Master Hongzhi's.

Despite the changes Zen has undergone, it is still part of the Ch'an tradition in the same way that Ch'an is part of Buddhism. Ch'an's roots are in Indian Buddhism, and the roots of Zen are in Ch'an.

The most famous sect of Korean Ch'an is the Chogye Order, which was transmitted to Korea during the Northern Sung Dynasty of China (960–1179). It is named after a location, *Caoxi* in Chinese, where the sixth Patriarch, Huineng, lived, in honor of him. Chogye is part of the Linji tradition. Before the Northern Sung Dynasty there were nine masters teaching Ch'an in Korea, but it is the lineage that became Chogye which survived. Ch'an was transmitted to Vietnam much later, in the Ming Dynasty.

This book is intended to introduce the living tradition of Ch'an teachings in order to help us release ourselves from suffering and give rise to wisdom and compassion. The Buddhadharma can teach us to make use of our opportunities in daily living in order to transform our outlook, our deeds, and our minds so that we can gain freedom from suffering, harmony in our lives, and ultimately, realize enlightenment.

To release ourselves from the suffering and dissatisfaction of our lives requires wisdom. At the same time, wisdom is necessary in order to be able to recognize the suffering and pain of others. Those who have gained wisdom will dedicate their lives to the benefit of others and create methods and situations so that other people will also be freed from their suffering, afflictions, and distress. Conversely, even if a person is lacking the genuine wisdom of Buddhism, if he or she can feel compassion and act with compassion for others, that person's own suffering and afflictions will naturally diminish, and his or her wisdom will increase. Wisdom and compassion are intimately intertwined.

Youthful Questioning

I would like to tell you about three events that happened to me when I was young, and that influenced me to follow the Buddhist path. Each of them raised questions about the nature of life.

As a child I was very sickly, and that slowed down my development both physically and educationally. I did not learn how to speak until I was about seven years old, and I did not begin reading until I was nine. I was always quiet, and not terribly bright.

Even though my family was poor, my

parents always helped people in need. They were Buddhist in the uneducated folk way of country people. We children were taught an accepting attitude toward life. My father would tell me, "Big ducks go the big duck way, and small ducks go the small duck way, so everyone has his or her own way to go." Beyond lessons such as that, I didn't think about "big" questions until I was about ten years old, when something happened that made me think about the nature of life for the first time.

In the flooded rice fields of the Chinese countryside, there were many water snakes. These snakes are not harmful, since they do not bite people and are not poisonous. No one, not even a child, is afraid of them, even though they can grow quite long. One day I saw a snake over a yard long pursuing a frog about the size of half of one's palm. When the snake had almost caught the frog, the frog turned and faced the snake. The snake also stopped, and darted his tongue out at the frog. Strangely enough, the frog moved toward the mouth of the snake, seeming to offer himself up. The snake snatched up the frog by the head and then gradually swallowed it whole. My first impulse was to save the frog, and I picked up a stick to hit the snake. But then I thought, "The snake needs to eat, just like other animals. To save the frog from the snake would be as if someone took my dinner out of my mouth." In saving the frog I'd be hurting the snake. It didn't seem right to interfere. But even though I had this moment of clarity about what was happening, I did not feel good about the whole thing.

I watched the shape of the frog travel from the mouth of the snake through the throat and into the body. It made a vivid impression. Because I could still see the frog, I wondered, "What happens to the frog? Do the frog and the snake merge into one life? If I were the frog, where would I be now?"

What also confused me was that the frog had clearly been afraid of the snake initially. He tried to escape and obviously did not want to be eaten. Why, then, did the frog finally crawl toward the mouth of the snake and let himself be eaten? I could not figure it out, and it left me deeply puzzled.

That same summer I had a second important experience. It was a busy year! I was in the rice fields with my elder brother, crossing a narrow bridge made of a single log, which were common in the Chinese countryside. A short distance under the bridge was a stream, and in the stream two water buffalo that belonged to a neighboring family were resting after their day's work in the fields. If the buffalo stood up, their heads were above the level of the bridge, but if they lay in the water, they were hidden beneath the bridge. When I crossed the bridge in one direction I did not see them, but when I came back, there they were. Water buffalo are big and might seem intimidating, but people in the countryside are used to them—they are domestic animals—so I was not afraid and started across the bridge. The buffalo looked at me and retreated a bit, but then they got very agitated and started spitting water all over. I had no idea what to make of this! Was it a sign of aggression, or perhaps a sign of welcome? I was frightened and didn't know what to do, and I froze in the middle of the bridge. Standing there, I finally became so terrified that I simply fell off the bridge right onto the head of one of the water buffalo. The buffalo, perhaps just as scared as I was, ducked under the water. Fortunately my elder brother was there and dragged me out.

After I'd had a chance to collect myself, two thoughts occurred to me. First, I observed that my fear of the water buffalo, instead of helping me get away from them, had resulted in my coming into closer contact with them. Were it not for my fear, I would not have fallen off the log. It seemed that something similar had happened to the frog, which, afraid for its life, had fled the snake. It is often true in life that you end up close to what you fear, try as you may to escape it. What you fear is what you must confront. I experienced this understanding as a kind of realization or awakening.

Second, I wondered what would have happened to me if I had died as a result of this accident, just as I had wondered what had happened to the frog. I couldn't figure that out at all. If I had drowned, where would I be? I kept thinking about this but couldn't come up with any answers. Questions about what would happen to me after I died bothered me for a long time after this incident.

As you might expect, I was also afraid of water buffalo for a long time; I suppose you might call it buffalophobia. Much later I understood that the essential reason I was afraid of buffalo was that I was afraid of death. I was afraid of death because I did not know what would happen to me after death. I overcame my fear of buffalo when I finally realized that death is really not a problem.

A third event that affected me greatly occurred after I left home to take up monastic life, when I was about thirteen years old. I was at Guangchao monastery, on Wolf Mountain in Chiangsu China, where there were less than fifty monks. One day I was to take part in an important ceremony performed jointly by three Dharma masters. Part of the ceremony was a purification ritual that required a willow branch or stick. My grand master said to me, "Little novice, go and fetch three identical willow branches, each with three leaves."

This seemed an easy task. I went and fetched three branches from the willow trees that drooped over a nearby river. When I showed them to my grand master he said, "These are not identical."

I said, perhaps a bit boldly, "They are identical in being willow."

My grand master said, "I want three branches which look identical." So I went back to the river, and to save myself further trouble I brought back a very big branch of willow, thinking that my grand master could choose from it the branches he wanted himself.

The master scolded me, and I went back to the river a third time. After a long search I found three willow branches that I thought looked very much the same. I took the branches back to the monastery and my grand master looked at them carefully and said, "They are not the same."

"But they are the same!" I responded with real frustration.

But my grand master pointed at the branches and said, "Look, the shape of this leaf is very thick, but the corresponding leaf on the other branch is thin. And the shapes of the branches do not look quite the same. Try again."

I was really angry. I thought of telling the grand master to go and look for himself, but of course I did not dare. I went back to the river and spent a long time there. I almost fell into the water trying to reach branches that were further out and looked the same from a distance. Unfortunately, once I got closer they never turned out to be the same.

Finally I gave up. I resigned myself to whatever punishment awaited me and returned empty-handed. My grand master did not seem the least bit bothered and simply said, "There are no two things really identical in this world. In the midst of sameness there is difference and in the midst of difference there is sameness. Take care of the willow branches you gathered before. We have to use them tomorrow." Though I was a little perplexed I felt great relief. My ordeal was finally over!

The next day at noon it was time for the ceremony, and the masters needed the three willow branches. When I went to get them I realized the branches had dried out. I should have left them in water, but I had not thought to do so. They were ruined, and of no use for the ceremony. I was certain my grand master was going to give me a beating, but he did not. He did ask me, "How dumb can you be?" but then he added, "Everything in this world is impermanent. I guess we'll have to use dried willow branches."

This incident revealed two things to me. I realized that no two things in this world are really identical. When seen from a distance things may appear to be the same, but upon closer observation one inevitably finds that they are not. First, my grand master asked me to find identical branches, and later he said that identical branches cannot be found. I don't know whether he intended to give me a lesson in Buddhism, but the incident was quite illuminating for me.

The second thing that had a great effect on me was my grand master's final comment. He said that nothing in the world is permanent. Everything is impermanent. It is not just that this is true most of the time, or that it is a truth to be considered alongside an equally valid notion of stability. Everything is always impermanent. It wasn't just that the willow branches had changed by the second day. At the very moment when I took them from the trees they were changing. They were always impermanent.

The two things I understood from my experience with the willow branches had a deep effect on me and gave me insights I have carried through life. To this day I do not think that other people should be like me or should think like me. I don't expect that any two individuals will be the same or that any two things will be identical. It is not possible, so why expect or desire it?

The experiences I had in my youth, the three stories I have told and the questions they aroused in me, are relevant to Ch'an practice. I tell them to you because they are a good introduction to understanding Ch'an, and they helped me begin my practice. But what exactly is their relevance to Ch'an practice? I will not tell you. It is something that you can investigate. In Ch'an you must always investigate for yourself.

2.

Who Was Buddha? What Is Ch'an?

WHO WAS BUDDHA?

Shakyamuni Buddha was born in a small kingdom in what is now Nepal in the sixth century B.C.E. Although the date of his birth is uncertain, East Asians generally celebrate it on April 8. In China we remember our mothers with gratitude on our birthdays, and in the same spirit, we should feel grateful to Buddha for giving us the chance to enter into the Dharma, the Buddha's teachings. We have selected one day out of the year on which to be thankful that such a being came into our world. Does a perfectly enlightened being like Buddha *need* a celebration in his honor? Of course not! It is for our own benefit that we celebrate his birthday.

When people asked me when I was born and whether I celebrate my birthday, I reply that every day and every moment can be regarded as my birthday. Happy occasions are always worth commemorating as our birthdays, because during those pleasant times we can say that we are indeed reborn. If we learn to appreciate the simple happiness in life, then every moment can be an occasion for celebrating our birthdays. We will feel that we are born again and again, always feeling new and happy.

There is nothing new about this perspective. Over two thousand years ago the Buddha said that every sentient being experiences birth and death in every moment. Our minds, bodies, and everything around us are continually being born and dying. All change constantly. This is "impermanence," a concept which is central to the Ch'an understanding of the intrinsic nature of ourselves and the world. For many people, old age and death seem to be sorrowful events, but even that sadness is constantly born and dies. If a person is to remain sad about death, he or she must constantly bring that sadness back into being. Each of our thoughts and actions is born and dies, and each action creates the seeds of consequences which will ripen in the future and give rise to new conditions of existence. This cycle of action and consequence is the cycle of karma. As we go through the processes of birth, aging, and death, we are constantly building our future through our actions and their consequences.

Buddhists believe that whatever we do in this life will plant karmic seeds that will result in our next birth and its conditions. Consequently, we should be careful of our actions of body, speech, and mind. If we know that at each moment we are creating something for the future, we should be happy. We have the opportunity to make our actions good so that the consequences will be good for us and for others. If we strive at every moment to work selflessly for the good of all beings, then we can truly speak of a new life at every moment.

On Buddha's birthday we offer him food and flowers, and we chant and perform ceremonies in his honor. Is the Buddha aware of this? It is we who enjoy the food and the flower arrangements, and it is we who derive benefit from the chanting and ceremonies. Where, then, is the Buddha? If he is unaware of our offerings, what is our purpose in doing these things? What is the purpose of remembering the historical Buddha as a person?

Do we remember the Buddha because some essence of him has remained behind for us? Some Buddhists believe that while the body of Shakyamuni Buddha perished thousands of years ago, his spirit remains. Is this correct according to Buddha's teachings? No, it is not. Everything changes and is impermanent, including both our spirits and our physical bodies. Buddhism maintains the view of *anatman:* it does not believe in a permanent soul or spirit.

The sutras tell us that Shakyamuni Buddha was born and lived for eighty years *because* beings in this world had developed a karmic affinity with him. "Karma" means "action" and, by extrapolation, the chain of cause and effect that Buddhists call "cause and consequence." Karmic affinity is an attraction, sympathy, and responsiveness that results from Buddha's and our actions, speech, and thoughts. Because we continue to have karmic affinity with his teachings, they continue to help us. The period of Buddha's life was only a partial expression of his compassionate acts, acts to relieve the suffering of sentient beings.[5] Buddha's historical life should not be considered his totality. During his life in India, he was known as Shakyamuni, but in fact Shakyamuni was only a transformation body of the Buddha.

If Shakyamuni Buddha was only a transformation body, a kind of incarnation, then there should be something more fundamental. That is called the Dharma body, the Dharmakaya, or the embodiment of truth. It takes the nature or "body" of every dharma, so it exists everywhere in time and space and is not separate from impermanent phenomena. It interacts with sentient beings everywhere in the universe; it is inseparable from sentient beings. If sentient beings have established an affinity with the Buddha, they realize this.

The Buddha can manifest in any form as a transformation body to help sentient beings. According to an Indian myth,

---

5. Buddhists traditionally differentiate between sentient beings, including animals but also gods, ghosts, etc., which experience suffering, and nonsentient living things like plants, which Buddhists traditionally believe do not experience pain and suffering.

Shakyamuni Buddha was the ninth incarnation of the god Vishnu. In China some people believe that Lao Tzu, the Taoist philosopher, was an incarnation of the Buddha. Some Westerners believe that Jesus was also an incarnation of the Buddha. Essentially, we can say that whenever a good person appears in the world to help sentient beings, this is another form or incarnation of Buddha. Buddhists do not restrict the phrase "the birth of the Buddha" to Shakyamuni. It can also describe the arising of any event or person that helps sentient beings to overcome suffering and ignorance. In a theoretical sense, anyone can be an incarnation of Buddha. So, in remembering the Buddha on his birthday we are in effect reminding ourselves of the potential that exists within each one of us.

The wisdom and compassion of the Buddha are accessible at any time and in any place. As long as we have established the proper karmic affinity with the Buddha through our good actions, it is possible for each of us to encounter Buddha's wisdom and compassion. This does not mean that we will encounter the form of the Buddha, but through an encounter with a person, an animal, or an event, we can receive the benefit of the Buddha's wisdom and compassion. Seen in this light, then, the date of Buddha's birthday does not matter at all. What is important is that we keep ourselves open to benefiting from the Buddhadharma. We can say that at any moment when we benefit from the Dharma, the Buddha is born.

It is through our mothers that we acquire our physical bodies, and so on our birthday we are grateful to our mothers. But how long will this physical body last? Even in the best circumstances, probably less than a hundred years. There is another kind of body called Dharma or wisdom body, which we can attain through the Buddhadharma. Our physical body is short-lived, but our accumulated wisdom will be carried on into the future through the working of cause and consequence: karma. The karmic seeds we plant now will bear fruit in the future. The beginning of our wisdom life can be very small. For instance, it can begin when we hear even one sentence of the Dharma and feel a little benefit from it. In the same way that a newborn infant will someday grow into an adult, so too the tiny seed of wisdom born as a consequence of hearing that one sentence will eventually blossom, and when it blossoms in action and thought, it will be the Buddha. In this sense, we can say that we each have our own individual Buddha's Birthday the moment when we start to feel benefit from the Buddhadharma. For those of you coming into contact with the Dharma for the first time, I would like to express my congratulations! This may be your Buddha's Birthday.

Shakyamuni Buddha was the first person in this world to attain complete enlightenment and spread the Dharma. So, in conventional terms, we speak of Buddha's Birthday as the birth-day of Shakyamuni Buddha. But if we think of the concept I just explained, then his birthday should be the moment when he first decided to practice, the first moment he began to cultivate the wisdom of the Dharma. From the time Shakyamuni Buddha began his practice until the time he experienced enlightenment under the Bodhi Tree, he constantly made progress, even if at times it was very slight. Every time such progress toward wisdom and compassion is made, we can consider that moment the rebirth of Shakyamuni Buddha.

When was the Buddha born? The Buddha *is* born when people like ourselves are open to him and can receive his help, his compassion, and his wisdom. The most important thing for us, after we receive a little of the Buddha's wisdom, is that we do something positive with the Buddha's teaching and allow the Dharma to help us change our attitude toward life. Even if the change is small, if it is for the better it is significant.

WHAT IS CH'AN?

Shakyamuni Buddha founded Buddhism, and Buddhism has been perpetuated through the Dharma, or Buddha's teachings; and the sangha: the community of *bhiksu* (monk) and *bhiksuni* (nun) practitioners. But what is Ch'an? Ch'an is a method of spiritual practice. Ch'an is wondrous and subtle, inexplicable wisdom. Ch'an is all phenomena.

Ch'an, understood as a spiritual practice, is a school of Buddhism that developed in China from Indian *dhyana* Buddhism, which Indian teachers introduced into China as early as the third century. The mental discipline and spiritual practices of *dhyana*, which aimed at attainment of an absorbed state of mind through concentration, were common to all Indian religions, including Hinduism and Buddhism, and are still used in yoga today. In China, *dhyana* was pronounced "ch'an," and its meditation techniques were avidly studied by the Chinese. Over time, however, Ch'an developed a different emphasis from that which *dhyana* had had in India. Ch'an later spread to other parts of Asia, and was called *Zen* in Japan, *Son* in Korea, and *Thien* in Vietnam.

Indian religions taught *dhyana* methods of meditation and concentration to allow people to emancipate themselves from their unsatisfactory spiritual condition: the afflictions, burdens, and troubles of the human mind. These vexations are caused by our desires, and the scattered condition of our thoughts makes it difficult to see and understand this. A person who is beginning Ch'an training needs to use the basic techniques of concentration to quiet and unify the mind. These include concentrating on the breath, on the body (for instance, on movements or the impurity of the body), and on sounds such as flowing water.

The purpose of concentration techniques is to take the mind away from a state of scattered thoughts and feelings of affliction and fetteredness, first to a state of concentration and then to a state where the separation between external and internal disappears. But this is only the first step in Ch'an practice. Ch'an does not depend on, and goes beyond, the *dhyana* techniques of concentration.

We can find instruction in the methods of Ch'an as a spiritual practice in the teachings of the patriarchs, the recognized and revered masters of old. Master Shandou (480–560) taught *dhyana* methods exactly as they had been transmitted from India. One such method was the Four Foundations of Mindfulness. First the practitioner meditates on the uncleanness or impurity of the body, for example on the digestive process. Next, she meditates on sensation, and the essentially suffering, unsatisfactory (*duhkha* in Sanskrit; *dukkha* in Pali) nature of sensation. Sensation is essentially *duhkha* because even pleasant sensations are conditioned and pass away. For instance, our happiness is conditional upon our health and the health of our families, our jobs, whether our country is at peace, and so on. All of these things are impermanent. Some experiences are inherently painful, and even the things we enjoy cause us suffering when we lose them.

Next, the practitioner meditates on the impermanent nature of mind and the absence of a true or permanent self as the center of one's psychophysical being.

The fourth meditation is on the impermanent nature of all dharmas, meaning all phenomena. This includes the three previous mindfulnesses.

The fourth Ch'an Patriarch, Daoxin (580–651) taught *dhyana* meditation techniques in *The Essential Practical Methods for Purifying the Mind*. He advised practitioners to begin the practice of Ch'an by simply observing the mind. He said to sit alone in a quiet place, straight and upright, in loose clothing so that you are not restricted. Let your body and mind relax completely, and then massage yourself from head to foot a few times. Adjust your body and mind so that they are in harmony, and observe your thoughts and feelings without becoming involved with them.

Daoxin also described the progressively deepening states of concentration a practitioner may pass through. First, the practitioner experiences both inner and outer worlds as empty and pure. He or she moves through deepening states of concentration until all thoughts disappear, and there is not even the thought of concentrating the mind. Finally, the practitioner transcends all mental realms of experience and goes beyond concentration to the unification of inner and outer. All distinctions are dissolved.

In every age and in every place, many methods of practice have been used. The techniques of Ch'an are flexible and adaptable. Because of changing situations and different types of people, a teacher uses a different method to lead each person toward enlightenment.

Once a layman asked the Sixth Patriarch, Huineng, "Isn't it necessary to practice meditation and *samadhi* in order to obtain emancipation?"

The Sixth Patriarch answered, "No. The Way [the intrinsic nature of reality] is realized by the mind. How can it exist in the act of sitting?"

Methods are only expedient means to clarify the mind. Therefore they must be used flexibly.

In the T'ang period (618–907), many famous masters used unusual techniques to lead people to enlightenment. Master Deshan Xuanjian (in Japanese: *Tokusan*, 781–867) was famous for hitting disciples with a stick. He was originally a Buddhist scholar and an expert on the *Diamond Sutra*, which is one of the most important texts in Ch'an. After an old lay woman made it clear to him with a single question that he did not understand the deeper meaning of the *Diamond Sutra*, he went to a monastery to dedicate himself to the investigation of Ch'an.[6] Eventually he assumed the leadership of the monastery on Mt. Deshan, and when he asked his disciples questions, whether they answered him or were silent, he hit them. These were not light taps but were sometimes very severe blows.

Linji Yixuan (*Rinzai*, d. 866/67), the founder of the Linji sect of Ch'an, helped his disciples by shouting at them. Zhaozhou (*Joshu*) simply told students to go and have a cup of tea. The eighth-century master Shigun answered "Watch me shoot this arrow" to all questions about Buddhism.

These Ch'an masters became famous for their unusual methods, but they did not use the same method mechanically for everyone. Deshan did not hit somebody who was not ready to benefit from his blow, and Linji did not shout at someone who was not ready to benefit from a shout. If a Ch'an master was so inflexible in his teaching methods, we would have to think him rather crazy.

Consider the ninth-century master, Huangbo Xiyun (*Obaku Kiun*, d. 850), whose writings have long been translated into English. Huangbo told his monks to eat all day long but never to bite into a grain of rice, and to walk all day long but never to tread on an inch of ground. He meant that we should never separate ourselves from the affairs of life, but we should also not allow ourselves to be controlled by our environment or external

6. Thomas Cleary and J. C. Cleary, trans., *The Blue Cliff Record* (Boston & London: Shambala, 1992); see Case 4, p. 22.

conditions. When we can do this, we are no longer attached to the self, and no longer hold on to the concept that the self and other people are distinct. Only a person who lives this way is truly free and at ease. A person who is free from attachment to the self is positively involved with life and does not react with confusion, anxiety, or suffering to events, other people, or the environment.

Huangbo emphasized that you can carry on spiritual practice in any situation. You do not have to leave society or become a *bhiksu*. This is the belief of Ch'an. If we can achieve the state of mind he described, then we will be deeply enlightened people, worthy of being great Ch'an masters.

In Ch'an, the *dhyana* techniques for developing concentration and entering into *samadhi* are generally used by beginners. An experienced practitioner rises above the necessity of such techniques. Ch'an itself is not ultimately technique or method, but rather it is the Way through which you attain by the application of the methods of practice. This brings us to the second definition of Ch'an: Ch'an is wondrous, subtle, and inexplicable wisdom.

Ch'an is inexplicable because we cannot express, describe, or explain it with words, nor can we imagine it or grasp it with our conceptual mind. Anything that we can express in language, no matter how wonderful, is not Ch'an.

The word "Ch'an" can mean enlightenment. Enlightenment, *kai wu,* which literally means "to open to awakening," can be understood as "the first meaning," "the ultimate meaning," or "the ultimate truth." In Ch'an there is also what is called "secondary meaning." Secondary meaning can be expressed in words and concepts, but the primary or ultimate meaning of Ch'an cannot. In the Ch'an tradition, the ultimate truth is sometimes compared to the moon, and the conventional truth to a finger pointing at the moon. Someone seeing the moon points in order to show it to people who haven't seen it yet. If they look at the finger, not the moon, they are not getting it. The finger is not the moon. Words, language, ideas, and concepts are like the finger; they can express only the secondary truth, but they can point to the ultimate truth. The ultimate truth is called mind, intrinsic nature, or Buddha nature. It is something everyone must experience personally. It can never be described.

Let's look at some examples of Ch'an masters pointing to Ch'an, within the limitations of language. The *Platform Sutra,* one of the most influential Ch'an texts, records the life and teachings of the Sixth Patriarch of Ch'an, Huineng. After his realization of the Dharma, Huineng received the Buddha's robe and bowl from the fifth Ch'an Patriarch. This symbolized that he was the Sixth Patriarch, giving him the authority to transmit the Dharma. Because he had held only a lowly position in the monastery, and the *bhiksus* had not known that he had any attainment, there was great controversy. Huineng was advised by the Fifth Patriarch to flee from the temple so that the others would not harm him out of jealousy. He set out for the mountains of southern China, where he would remain for ten years.

Some *bhiksus* chased him, however, including Huiming, a former general who was both strong and strong-willed. When Huiming caught up with him, the Sixth Patriarch put the Buddha's robe and bowl, the symbols of the Dharma transmission, on a rock, and said, "Here, take them. I don't want to fight with you over these things."

Huiming tried to pick them up but could not move them. Surprised and impressed, he said, "I did not come for the robe and the bowl, I came for the Dharma."

Huineng then delivered his first teaching as a Dharma master. He asked Huiming, "Not thinking of good or evil, who is it that stands before me?" This is still a good question for us today. Can *you* answer it?

Master Baizhang Huaihai, (*Hyakujo*, 720–814) pointed to Ch'an as inexplicable wisdom when he said to a *bhiksu*, "Say something to me without using your mouth, your throat, or your lips."[7]

Baizhang expressed the same idea in a different way when he said that the true wisdom of Buddha is attained when you are no longer restricted by any concepts, including good and evil, impurity and purity, techniques, methods, spiritual blessings, and worldly concerns. If you can transcend all attachment to concepts, you have achieved the true wisdom of the Buddha. Baizhang includes *fu*, which refers specifically to the obtaining of merit by good acts, in his list of concepts we must transcend.

7. Ibid.; Case 70, p. 391.

This is a common concept for Chinese Buddhists to be attached to, even today.

Ch'an is a form of spiritual practice, Ch'an is inexplicable wisdom, but Ch'an is also all phenomena. There is nothing that is not it, and there is no place where it is not. Shakyamuni Buddha said that all dharmas are Buddhadharma. We can also say, "All dharmas are the Dharma of Ch'an." "Dharma" with a small *d* means phenomena, including people, things, events, ideas, time, space, etc. "Dharma," with a capital D means the law, in the sense of natural law, and it means the Buddha's teachings. Even though Ch'an transcends all concepts, and all things that can be grasped or defined, Ch'an excludes absolutely nothing.

Zhaozhou (*Jo-Shu*, 778–897—yes, he lived over a hundred years) shows us this in a koan:

One day, a *bhiksu* studying in the temple of Zhaozhou, came to the master and said, "I am confused and ignorant, please give me some direction and teaching."

Zhaozhou asked, "Did you eat your porridge yet?"

The *bhiksu* answered, "Yes, I have."

The master said, "Then go and wash your bowl."[8] Upon hearing that, the *bhiksu* realized enlightenment.

If you drank a glass of milk and I said to you, "Please go and wash your glass," do you think you would have an enlight-

8. Robert Aitken, *The Gateless Barrier* (San Francisco: North Point Press, 1990); see Case 7, p. 54.

enment experience? There are probably parents all over the world who are saying that to their children today. Are the children becoming enlightened? We have to remember the background of a story like this; the *bhiksus* had probably been practicing for a long time. The mind of a person with long practice is straightforward and very pure.

Anything that we do *can* be considered to be Ch'an practice. Nothing that we do is excluded from practice. But it is also not quite so simple.

In another story a *bhiksu* asked a master, "What is Ch'an?"

The master answered, "When you're hungry, eat; when you're tired, go to bed."

Upon receiving this instruction, the *bhiksu* said, "Everybody eats when they're hungry and sleeps when they're tired. Does that mean that everybody is in a Ch'an state?"

The master answered, "When you are eating, are you eating with a completely unified mind? When you are sleeping, aren't you also having all kinds of dreams?"

In another famous story, a *bhiksu* said to Master Zhaozhou, "All dharmas [meaning all things] return to the One. Where does the One return to?" All dharmas returning to the One refers directly to practice, where we concentrate the scattered mind and attain the state of one mind. When we talk of that oneness returning to something, it sounds similar to the religious concept that everything comes from and returns to God.

Master Zhaozhou answered, "When I was in Ching Province I had a robe made for me that weighed seven pounds." He had been asked a profound, abstract, philosophical question, but he gave a prosaic, obscure-seeming answer. It may appear that the question was not addressed by his response. But look more closely. Zhaozhou's meaning was simple. All he was saying was that he had returned from Ching with a nice new robe and he was pleased with it. Whatever anybody had asked him, he would have said, "I just had this new robe made."[9]

You don't have to use philosophical concepts in order to inquire into truth. The question of where the One returns to is not important. The most brilliant philosopher as well as the most unskilled laborer has to eat and sleep and go to the bathroom. Why do we tend to think there is some truth that is limited only to the brilliant philosopher? Ch'an is not opposed to philosophical inquiry, or to brilliance, but we do not have to use sophisticated concepts and ideas in order to seek the ultimate truth. That ultimate truth is all around us and right before us at all times, in our everyday ordinary lives.

What is the meaning of these examples? Whatever you do, however ordinary, whatever you see before you is nothing other than Ch'an. But nothing in itself is the whole of Ch'an.

THE CH'AN VIEW OF LIFE

Up to this point we have been looking at Ch'an itself, but what is the Ch'an view of our lives and the purpose of our lives?

There are several levels of view, or understanding, of life in

9. Cleary and Cleary, *The Blue Cliff Record*, Case 45, p. 270.

Ch'an, because Buddhism recognizes that each individual's view of life depends on his or her perspective and level of development. If you see deeply into things, then that's your understanding. If you see only what is shallow, then that is your understanding. Ch'an is all phenomena. In other words, all things great and small are in accord with the teachings of Ch'an. This is a deep view of life, and few of us can grasp it.

If your view of life is that it has no goal or purpose, you will probably feel that life is empty and meaningless. If your life seems to have no meaning, you may wonder, "Why do I bother to live?" You may feel that you are nothing but a drain on earth's resources.

Confucius said, "Food and sex, these are the human instincts." That is, the desire to continue to exist and the urge to procreate comprise the animal side of human nature. This is the lowest view of human life, and we can call it the animal view of life. Life is just a search for food, shelter, and procreation, as it is for an animal. It has no other purpose. Is this your attitude?

A variation on this view of life is to believe that human existence is spontaneous, without cause or purpose. People with this view drift and let situations determine themselves. Do you recognize that there are people who live their lives according to these animal-level understandings of life?

We might term a second view of life the "deluded" or "foolish" perspective. This is a slight step above the animal view. People with this view believe that what is important is to fight and struggle for safety and security. They accumulate wealth and seek power and position in order to protect their security and that of their descendants.

In ancient times an important government official paid a visit to an unusual *bhiksu* who lived in a tree. It was not uncommon for an official of that time to seek guidance from a *bhiksu*. Chinese officials were chosen by examination, and most were highly educated and cultured people. Many Buddhist *bhiksus* and masters were also educated people, and they were wise, so their lectures and guidance attracted officials. Even emperors sought the guidance of Ch'an masters.

As I said, this master lived in a tall tree. The official said to him, "Master, you are in a very dangerous situation."

The master answered, "I am not in any danger. You, however, are in a dangerous situation."

The official asked, "How can I be in a dangerous situation? I am head of the local government. I am protected by many people. How can my situation be dangerous?"

The master said, "Earth, water, fire, and wind constantly vex you [these are the elements that the Chinese of that time believed made up all physical phenomena]. The processes of birth, sickness, old age, and death can affect you at any time. Greed, anger, ignorance, and arrogance are your constant company. How can you claim that you are not in a dangerous situation?"

The official was intelligent and had good karmic roots (karmic potential) for wisdom. He understood immediately and said, "Master, indeed, I am in a position far worse than yours."

Human beings are deluded. In this world, there is no truly safe place.

A person with a deluded view of life is like a dog chasing his own tail, believing that it is another dog. He chases his tail around and around a tree, thinking, "Just let me get that dirty dog!" He will never catch his own tail, just as wealth, power, success, and prestige will never guarantee our security. Eventually the dog dies, as do we. When the dog dies, he does not know what life was about or why he dies. He is unaware that he has been chasing his own tail. Such is the deluded view of life, and many, many of us live this way.

If the view that the purpose of life is to struggle for safety and security is deluded, what view does a wise person hold? Here we are speaking about worldly wisdom, and we mean someone who lives according to principled ideals and goals. Most of us like to believe we fall into this category.

An example of a person with worldly wisdom is the artist who is devoted to beauty and its rendering. The process of creating a work of art can be painful, but when the work is finished, seeing or hearing it can be a beautiful experience, both for the creator and the audience. In the process the artist may be beautified, and so also the world. The artist's internal experience of beauty may transform the environment. While she is at work, inside and outside are not experienced as separate. The artist recognizes that the whole universe is one creative work of art.

Often the world seems beautiful to the artist while he is creatively involved, but when he must deal with the ordinary world, life may not seem so wonderful. I know a painter whose work is truly beautiful. He is happy when he talks about paintings and art with other people. But when the conversation shifts away from art, he becomes irritable and bad-tempered. He makes life difficult for his wife and friends.

Artists may experience beautiful moments, moments of non-separation of self and not-self, but these are transitory. Life is not always beautiful. More often than not, it is the not-so-beautiful aspects of ordinary life that we experience.

Some scientists, whose lives are devoted to the analysis and observation of the physical world, also exhibit the wise view of life. They experience the limitlessness of nature and from that extrapolate the limitlessness of what is within them. They may observe only matter, but with their keen understanding they see an unlimited totality. Can they use science to discover the meaning of life? That is unlikely.

A scientist once said to me, "Shih-fu, science and Buddhism reach the same conclusion, so if I pursue science, there is no need to study Buddhism."

I said, "What conclusion is that?"

"Buddhism," he said, "says that there is no limit to phenomena. Science has also come to the same conclusion. Buddhism says all phenomena are empty, and science, in its analysis of matter at the most minute level, also finds no permanent substance. The conclusions are identical."

I responded, "No, they are completely different. Can science tell you why you were born into this world?"

He said, "Oh, that's simple. My mother gave birth to me."

I asked, "Why did your mother give birth to you and not to someone else?"

"My mother gave birth to me, and that's enough. It was not necessary that she have a different child."

I asked, "Then why were you born to this mother and not another?" He had no answer for that, so I said, "This shows that you are unclear about such fundamental questions: you do not have the answers." Finally, I asked, "Why have you come into this world and this life? Where will you go from here?"

Science may show us that phenomena are limitless and empty, but it cannot answer questions about the purpose of human life and what will happen to us after death. That is why many scientists come to adopt a religious faith or believe in God or another deity. Even Einstein was religious. In Taiwan, scientists often become Buddhists, because science cannot answer the fundamental questions about human existence.

Philosophers may also be wise. They live according to well-conceived ideas, and they consciously strive to incorporate their ideals and principles into daily living.

The religious constitute another group who seek wisdom. A religious person lives his life according to principles and recognized goals, and governs his life according to his faith. The meaning of his life is based on obeying God's law and on the anticipation of joining God in his heavenly kingdom after death.

The individual and God are, on the one hand, connected together; on the other hand, they are independent. This remedies a weakness of the artist, the scientist, and the philosopher, who run the risk of losing their identity in merging with their art, science, or philosophy. However, a person who believes in God sees himself as having an independent eternal identity, or soul. For many people it is important to have this sense of identity. Otherwise they feel empty.

The Ch'an view of life is different from that of worldly wisdom. The Ch'an view is that life's purpose is enlightenment, the letting-go of the self. We must pass through three stages to arrive at the dissolution of the self. First, we must affirm ourselves; second, mature ourselves; and third, dissolve ourselves. This is called the realistic view of human life, because it is grounded in ultimate reality.

To affirm oneself is to affirm the purpose, goal, meaning, and worth of one's life, and to be willing to look at oneself honestly and clearly. People ask, "Why were we born into this world and this life?" The Buddhist view is that we are here to receive our karmic retribution, and also to fulfill our aspirations or vows.

We must understand that in one lifetime our actions, both good and bad (which create karmic retribution), and the results of those actions (retribution), are relatively limited compared to the myriad of lives we have lived. What we do and what we receive in the present often do not correspond. Some people seem not to have done much good, and yet are born with wealth or find easy success. Others work hard their whole lives, yet can barely feed themselves. They achieve nothing, have unfulfilling relationships, and seem to live lives filled with suffering.

Why are there such disparities? To answer this, we must understand karmic retribution. This lifetime was preceded by innumerable previous lifetimes, during which we acted in many different ways. The consequences of these actions reach into this lifetime and future lifetimes until all the results of those actions have occurred. Then we will have received the full karmic retribution for the good and bad we have done. One reason we were born is to repay karmic debt from previous lifetimes. What passes from one lifetime to another? The karmic seeds we have planted: the actions we have done, both good and bad, which have not yet borne fruit.

I myself was born with many physical problems and was often sick as a child. I asked myself, "Why is my health so poor? Was my mother unfair, bringing a healthy brother and sister into the world, and me so sickly?" Now I understand that this was not my mother's doing. She had no choice. Our body at birth is the result of previous karmic seeds. But many of us feel that where and when we were born, and our whole lot in life, are unfair.

We have also come into this world to fulfill our aspirations and vows. A "vow" in Buddhism is the strongest promise or pledge that one can make.

Every one of us has aspirations and has made pledges and vows. Isn't that true? And haven't we all also made many promises that we didn't keep? People in love promise all sorts of things, but they often forget them once they are married. Any promise not fulfilled will eventually have to be repaid. We enter the world to fulfill our obligations and repay our debts.

Thus far, I have spoken about affirming the self. After we affirm ourselves, we must bring ourselves to maturity.

The process of maturing involves both leaving behind concern for yourself and reorienting yourself to the benefit of other sentient beings. Then you will be ready to bear inconvenience, trouble, and suffering on others' behalf. To save sentient beings from suffering, as Buddhists vow to do, requires that you give whatever is needed—time, money, or all your effort. When you give, it may seem that you lose something, but that is only the view of selfishness. A bodhisattva, an enlightened being, has no thought of loss or gain. It is the well-being of other sentient beings that is important.

To voluntarily abandon your own benefit, to actively help, and, when necessary, to suffer for the sake of sentient beings, is the correct attitude, or "right view." When our actions in the interest of others are voluntary, our own suffering diminishes. It is when suffering and vexation are involuntary that they are difficult to bear. Those on the Bodhisattva Path, even if they are only at the beginning, must disregard their own benefit despite the discomfort this may bring. If the sentient beings we help do not express gratitude, we should have no regrets. This is wisdom and compassion.

Finally, we must transcend the self. This third and final stage of development, according to Ch'an, is complete freedom from the self. After we have completely let go of the self, we return the benefit of our achievement to society and the world. We offer everything, whatever we own and whatever we have achieved, to all beings. Sentient beings may benefit from our efforts, but we experience no loss or gain. This is no-self, the stage of deep enlightenment.

If you realize deep enlightenment you will no longer need to listen to me talk about views of life, because you will no longer have a particular view of life. In Ch'an, the final, transcendent view of life is no view of life at all. What is there, then, to be said? To have a view of life is the condition of ordinary people. To transcend this concept is the condition of the deeply enlightened. Such people rise to whatever task is at hand.

There are many Ch'an gongans (in Japanese: koans) that illustrate this point. In one a monk asked, "What is the place where not one single blade of grass grows?"[10]

The master answered, "When you step outdoors, every place is full of fragrant grass." And then he added, "You can go all over the world, and you will see no fragrant grass."

I can rephrase the question as, "Where is the one place where you cannot see a single blade of grass?"

The answer is very special and seems quite strange. "No matter where you look, fragrant grass is everywhere," followed by, "You may walk all over the world, but you will see no fragrant grass." If every place is filled with fragrant grass, then you will not recognize it or give it a name. For example, if every being in this world is a dog, then there will be no reason to call anything "dog." The reality of life is apparent everywhere. Ch'an is all phenomena, and all dharmas are Buddhadharma. It

---

10. A similar story is recorded in William F. Powell, trans., *The Record of Tung Shan* (Honolulu: University of Hawaii Press, 1986), Case #73, p. 48, and in Thomas Cleary, trans., *Book of Serenity* (Hudson, NY: Lindisfarne Press, 1988), Case #89, p. 382.

is just a matter of realizing it. But if you purposefully look for the reality of life, you will never find it.

Another *gongan* tells about two Ch'an monks who were traveling and passed by an isolated, deserted temple. One monk needed to urinate, so he urinated in the temple hall, in front of the Buddha statue. The other monk scolded him: "Look, the Buddha is here. How can you urinate here?"

The first monk said, "Tell me where Buddha is not, and I'll urinate there."

The other monk said, "Buddha is everywhere."

The first monk happily said, "In that case, I can urinate everywhere."

If the reality of life is apparent everywhere, you may wonder why we develop the animal view of life, the deluded view of life, and even the view of worldly wisdom. In Buddhism we speak of "ignorance without beginning." The concept of "without beginning" is something that is unique to Buddhism. In general, philosophies and religions speak of a beginning or a first cause, but Buddhism does not. Buddhism speaks of "beginninglessness." When people asked, "Where does this 'beginninglessness' come from?" Shakyamuni Buddha himself chose to remain silent and give no reply. How could I dare to try to answer? To try to address this question intellectually is a trap. Only wisdom answers it.

3.

Buddhism, Pain, and Suffering

Buddhism grew out of Shakyamuni Buddha's search for the reasons for illness, old age, and death, the universal causes of *duhkha*. *"Duhkha,"* in Sanskrit, is often translated as "suffering." It includes the idea that life is impermanent and is experienced as unsatisfactory and imperfect. There are three classes of *duhkha*. The first is ordinary suffering, such as not getting what we desire or enduring what we do not like. The second is unsatisfactoriness caused by change, such as when a sensual pleasure or enjoyable meditation state ends. The third is *duhkha* caused by the conditioned, or impermanent, nature of all things and states, so that our very nature as ever-changing beings causes us *duhkha*.

Pain and suffering, *duhkha*, begin at birth and go on until we die. Physical illness and injury cause pain. The mind causes *duhkha*. Buddhadharma does not rid us of pain, it is not an anesthetic. But it can alleviate our suffering. Buddha said that we should see a doctor for physical illness and injury, but mental suffering should be treated with Buddhadharma.

Buddha saw that it was more important to save the mind than the body. Someone with a healthy body but whose mind is not at peace will suffer more than someone who has only physical problems. Someone who has a peaceful mind and a good attitude will be less afflicted by physical difficulties when they occur than someone whose mind is disturbed. If our mental problems and illusions are cured, that is liberation.

An English psychologist told me that he had heard something of great use and benefit to him during a recent retreat. I asked him what it was, and he said, "Every evening when we chant the evening service we say, 'To know all the Buddhas of the past, present, and future, perceive that Dharmadhatu nature [the phenomenal universe] is all created by the mind.' This understanding is of great use because, for example, when my legs hurt, I do not have to be afraid of the pain. When I accept the pain and do not dwell on it, it often goes away. Instead of pain there is a sensation of comfortable coolness. Whatever problems you have, if you face the problems, they will diminish."

He added that in the past he used talk therapy or drugs to

try to help his clients get rid of their problems. He didn't understand that when you accept a problem, that in itself is a way of resolving the problem. I asked him if he thinks this approach is useful for everybody. He thought about it and said, "Probably only for those with willpower and determination."

Even though this method may not work for everyone, the principle behind it is valid. That is, there are no problems that exist objectively per se. Problems have to exist in your own mind and perception. When there are no problems in your mind, objective problems do not exist. For this reason Buddhadharma considers other religions and philosophies "outer schools." They consider many problems and other phenomena to have an existence outside of one's own mind. From the Buddhist point of view, these things exist within one's mind.

That everything is created by our minds is not easy to grasp. In order to understand it, we must distinguish two levels of the mind. The conceptual mind is a shallow level of mind. It is influenced by what we've learned, how we feel, and so on, and is very conditioned. We cannot say that *it* is the cause of everything that happens to us or of the environment. However, fundamental mind, empty mind, the ultimate subject in all times, past, present, and future, truly gives rise to all phenomena, and to our problems. From the point of view of that empty mind, we can say that external problems are our own creation. We may not know that we have created those problems because they are hidden in the deeper level of mind.

Everything is created by the mind. You have your heaven and I have mine. You have your hell and I have mine. You may see me in your heaven and I may see you in my heaven, but nonetheless your heaven is different from mine. And it is the same with everything else.

If two married people spend twenty-four hours a day together, sharing the same bed and the same job, are they in the same world or in different worlds? The two of them encounter different physical matter, so even the physical worlds they inhabit are not identical. If I sit on this chair, you cannot sit on it. You have to sit somewhere else. If we eat together, even though we have the same dishes in front of us, what I eat and how much I eat is different from what you eat. You may find it delicious and I may find it not so great. You may find the same dish good today and not so good tomorrow.

Two individuals can live in the same world only if they have exactly the same mind. In meditation we call this having the one-mind state. If a person's mind is scattered, it is impossible to experience the same world as someone else.

Our suffering is caused by our minds. According to Buddhism, there are three conditions of mind that commonly cause suffering. The first is ignorance of no-beginning. Western religions talk about a beginning and Western science theorizes about the beginning of the universe, but the Buddha said that there is no beginning. Looking for a beginning is like looking for the starting point of a circle. Try as you might, you cannot find it. Thus we have no-beginning. If you ask, "Where does suffering come from?" a Buddhist will answer, "It has no beginning." So we cannot eliminate suffering by finding its beginning.

The second cause of suffering is ignorance of the cause/

effect cycle of suffering, which Buddhists call "cause and consequence." The effect that we suffer now is the result of previous
causes. This effect in turn becomes the cause for a future effect.
As we move forward in time, we incessantly create future causes
and future effects. We create our future suffering by what we do
now. "Karma" means action, and it refers to both cause and
consequence as they produce each other in this cycle. Buddhism
does not believe in any permanent, unchanging soul or spirit,
but holds that some karmic seeds planted by our actions in this
life will be reborn in order to bear fruit in another life. The
causes and effects, driven by desire, are, themselves, states of
suffering.

Vexations are the third cause of suffering. "Vexation" is a
special term in Buddhism, a translation of *klesa* in Sanskrit.
Vexations may arise from contact with the environment. For
instance, if we get wet in the rain we may get sick. Microbes that
cause diseases and pollutants can also make us sick and cause us
vexations. Heat and cold may bother us.

Vexations also arise from our relationships with other people. Most people think their enemies are responsible for most of
their vexations, but this is not necessarily the case. The people
with whom we quarrel most are often not our enemies but those
closest to us: our spouses, our children, our coworkers. Each day
we must deal not only with our close relations but with many
other people as well. Some we know, some we don't. Some help
us, some hinder us. And people compete endlessly with one
another.

Another source of vexations is our own emotional turmoil.

Our greatest enemy is not to be found on the outside; we are bothered most by our own minds. Our feelings constantly change. We may move from arrogance to regret, or from joy to sorrow, but we never look at something in the same way as time passes. We are in conflict with ourselves. We worry about gain and loss, right and wrong, and we cannot decide what to do. This is true misery. It is only when there is no grasping or rejecting that there will be neither lack nor excess.

What should we do about all the problems created by our minds? When we experience suffering, it helps to try to analyze its nature. Suffering can come in the form of greed, anger, ignorance, arrogance, or doubt. When we can reflect on the nature of our suffering, we can greatly reduce its intensity. Note that Buddhism is not concerned with the causality of a person's delusion and suffering. It is concerned only with their recognition and elimination. The power to do that is within the mind of the individual.

Greed is the desire to get what we want. An example of greed is the urge to conquer. People suffering from this desire want to increase what they have and to extend their influence. Some strive for fame while others use power to directly conquer those who oppose them. Power struggles caused by this desire may occur among nations or within families. A wife may try to conquer a husband or vice versa. Such desire to overpower others is, indeed, self-centered.

When greed causes us to suffer, we should reflect: "I am greedy, I have strong desires. This is the source of my suffering." Then the vexation of greed will diminish.

When we suffer from anger, we may reflect: "Why am I so angry? My distress is directly related to my anger." In this way the anger and distress will begin to subside. Look inward, not outward. It is not the "problem," but your own mind that you examine.

When we have done something ignorant, it will help alleviate our suffering and vexation if we recognize our error. Ignorance includes not understanding and accepting impermanence; in other words, believing we can hold on to things.

Arrogance is caused by believing that our achievements are entirely a result of our own abilities and wonderfulness, and not of causes and conditions. This attitude is clearly self-centered. Arrogance may lead to callousness and a general disregard for others. An arrogant person may believe that he or she has the right to hurt others or sweep them aside according to personal whim.

Despair caused by failure to achieve one's desired goals is the obverse of arrogance. Someone with this disturbance will lose all confidence in him- or herself and will also often blame others.

To recognize arrogance and despair, and their source in self-centeredness, and to be aware of the suffering they cause when we experience them, will help us to overcome them.

Doubt is also a type of vexation and a cause of suffering. Doubt prevents us from making decisions. It makes it impossible to trust others and to trust ourselves. This is, indeed, suffering! If you know you suffer from doubt, you should reason as follows: "I want to accomplish such and such task, so I had better believe that I have the ability and that it is the right thing to do." If you can believe this, you will be able to give yourself to what you wish to do.

Doubt can have a terrible influence on our lives. Imagine that you have decided to marry but you are plagued by doubt. You wonder if the marriage will end in divorce. Will your spouse abandon you after you are married? Did your partner lie, or has he or she withheld something important from you? If your doubt is unchecked, you will be miserable as you prepare for marriage and miserable within the marriage. Even if there is no real cause for you and your spouse to break up, doubt itself can furnish a reason.

If you suffer from such doubts, you should say to yourself, "If I have so many doubts, it would be foolish for me to marry. If I want to marry, I should accept my spouse as he or she is and trust him or her absolutely." If you cannot maintain such an attitude, marriage will only bring you misery.

Are there any of you who have no doubts? I have yet to meet someone who has absolutely none.

People often use two ineffective methods to try to alleviate their suffering. The first is denial: "I am not suffering. I have no problems. There is nothing wrong with me." As they protest that they have no problems, they may throw tantrums and work themselves into states of extreme agitation. I once asked some-one like that why he had so many vexations. "It's not me!" he cried, "It's these other rotten people who are making me so miserable." Actually, he had many problems that were of his own making.

Recently I was riding in a car with four people who were involved in a heated discussion. One said to me, "I'm sorry that we argue so much, Shih-fu."

I replied, "You're the ones arguing, it's really none of my business." Did I hear what they said? Yes, I did. But I was simply not part of the conversation.

Later another one of the four said to me, "I cannot stand to hear people argue. It upsets me." You might think that he was reacting to something outside himself. In fact, he caused his own vexation. It came from within him.

Another way people try to alleviate their own suffering is by continually reviewing a list of their faults and problems, and what they believe to be the remedies. This builds one false assumption on another. Both of these methods only make matters worse.

How can we alleviate suffering and bring peace to our minds? The Buddhist method of healing suffering is divided into two broad categories: change of concepts, or establishing right view; and methods of practice.

There are three important Buddhist concepts that can help us reduce our suffering. The first is the concept of cause and effect, which I mentioned earlier. While this concept is a religious belief, it is also a fact. Throughout our lives, no matter what we do, we observe responses to and effects of our actions. For instance, when we speak harshly to someone, they often respond harshly. Through faith, Buddhists believe that there was a life before this life and one before that, and so on through innumerable past lives. Much of what we experience now may seem unfair, but it is simply a consequence of actions performed in the past. To the extent that we believe this, we will be willing to accept the good and bad that befall us.

An understanding of the second important Buddhist concept, causes and conditions, can also help us reduce our suffering. All phenomena arise and pass away because of the accumulation and interaction of *many* different factors. The cause of a flower is the seed, but soil, water, and sun must also be present for the plant to come into existence. Time or uprooting or lack of water or sun will cause the seed to wither and die. The same is true for everything we do and everything that happens to us.

When we have succeeded in something, there is no need for us to be particularly excited or arrogant. No matter how much we have accomplished, it was not without the direct or indirect help of many other people. And since we know that all that is now coming into being will one day pass away, there is no need to despair when we encounter adverse or unfavorable conditions. They, too, will change. With a calm mind we will pass through good times and bad without undue unhappiness or elation. This is a sign of mental well-being.

The importance of the cultivation of compassion is the third concept that will help us alleviate our suffering. People usually wish others to be compassionate toward them, but the idea seldom occurs to them to be compassionate toward others. There are those who demand to be forgiven when they make a mistake: "Don't measure me against the standards of a saint!" they say. But if they see someone else err, they will say, "You're incompetent. Why can't you do anything right?!"

There are four components of compassion. The first is that we understand our own conflicts and the development of inner peace. The others are: sympathy for other people's shortcomings, forgiveness of other people's mistakes, and concern with other people's suffering. The first component of compassion allows us to develop the other components. In order to be at peace with yourself, you must have a calm and peaceful mind. To do this, keep in mind the concepts of cause and effect and causes and conditions. This will help you remain calm and peaceful, and you will then be able to be compassionate, sympathetic, forgiving, and caring toward others.

The second method of alleviating suffering is through the Buddhist methods of practice, including formal meditation, mindfulness, chanting, prostrating, and other methods of practice used in everyday life. Practice helps the concepts of cause and effect, causes and conditions, and compassion to take deep root in our lives.

4.

修行 Ch'an Training

Before the Chinese revolution in 1949, when I left home to live in a monastery, there were many Ch'an monasteries in China, but most were not the grand communities you might imagine. Monasteries could have as few as three *bhiksus* or *bhiksuni* (monks or nuns who have taken all of the precepts) or as many as several hundred. In general, *bhiksus* and *bhiksuni* lived in separate monasteries, and the monasteries for women were governed by abbesses. In most of the monasteries the Buddha statues took up more space in the main hall than was left for the *bhiksus* to stand in, so in monasteries with big "sanghas" (the community of practitioners) all the *bhiksus* could not even fit into the hall for services! In fact, few monasteries had a Ch'an Hall for meditation or a regular program of Ch'an training.

All monasteries were governed by the same rules, and daily life at each was much the same. *Bhiksus* and *bhiksuni* received two kinds of training. The first type was through the activities of daily life. Great emphasis was placed on carrying out one's monastic duties correctly, from manual labor to officiating at services to serving as abbot of a monastery. Also included in daily life training were performing rituals at prescribed times of the day, and daily meditation.

The second kind of training occurred during the periods of time set aside for intensive Ch'an retreats. The shortest of these meditation retreats were a week long, and there were others of twenty-one days, forty-nine days, and three months. The shorter retreats could be held in any of the Ch'an monasteries in China with the local abbot presiding. For retreats of twenty-one or forty-nine days, a local monastery would invite an eminent Ch'an master to preside, generally the abbot or the head of the Ch'an Hall from one of the great monasteries. The two most famous Ch'an masters of that time were Master Xuyun (Empty Cloud) and Master Laiguo. Both of these teachers had great impact on the practice of Ch'an, and on my own practice.

Master Xuyun lived from 1840 to 1959, one hundred and nineteen years, and was one of the great modern Ch'an masters.

He is famous for his own meditation practice, for his teaching of meditation, and for his revival of Ch'an monasteries and practice. After the Sung Dynasty (960–1279) the vitality of Ch'an gradually declined. Master Xuyun revived the practices of the five schools of Ch'an that had existed during the T'ang Dynasty (618–907) by transmitting the practices of each school to disciples who, in turn, spread them. Despite the communist revolution in China, these schools of Ch'an have survived. For instance, Master Sheng Yi, who now teaches in Hong Kong, received transmission of the Weiyang school of Ch'an from Master Xuyun. His monastery has continued many Ch'an traditions, including the tradition of forty-nine-day retreats. I myself received transmission in the Linji (known in Japan as *Rinzai*) school from Master Ling Yuan, who received transmission from Master Xuyun.

Master Xuyun was greatly respected and trusted, and because of the esteem all kinds of people had for him, he was able to act as a leader outside of religious matters. For instance, he once negotiated a truce in a war between a bandit band and the local militia. Bandits in China at that time were like the outlaw gangs of the American West. One band wanted control of a village that the militia was supposed to protect. Master Xuyun risked his life to talk to the bandits in order to save the people in the area from death and the hardships of war.

Master Xuyun helped people all over China to feel hopeful and positive about the Dharma and about their own capacity to practice. Over fifty monasteries were rebuilt with his encouragement, and more than a million people took refuge with him, thus formally committing themselves to Buddhist practice. (Taking refuge is similar to the Christian practice of baptism.)

Master Laiguo (1881–1953) was famous for his meditation practice and teaching. He was abbot of the Gaoming monastery in Zhejiang Province, which has been famous for Ch'an practice and retreat for over a thousand years. There, Master Laiguo trained both monks and laypeople using primarily the *hua to* method (see the section on methods of practice). He also wrote a book that teaches Ch'an practice step-by-step. Master Laiguo is also known for the quality of his disciple descendants, including Master Guangxian, who taught at Pu Chao Temple in New York City and has a temple in Fujian Province in China.

After this great Buddhist revival in the early twentieth century, you may wonder what has happened to Buddhist practice in mainland China since the revolution. Today practice is tolerated, but public lectures on Buddhism are not allowed. Masters, *bhiksus, bhiksuni,* and laypeople may only answer private questions in a one-on-one situation. In such a climate it is not surprising that bootleg books and tapes by Chinese masters circulate secretly among people who are interested in Buddhism, since they are the best source of information. When I went to China in 1996, I was allowed in only on the condition that I obey the ban on public speaking. Even a discussion held at the end of the trip among the three hundred people who accompanied me was stopped by a government official in charge of "public safety." Despite all of these restrictions, I nonetheless met some people who had heard of me through books and tapes!

In the large monasteries that existed when I was a boy, there were generally two three-month retreats each year, in summer and winter. Winters are too cold to travel or meditate alone in the mountains, so winter was a good time to gather at a monastery for group meditation. Summer is too hot to work, so it was also set aside for meditation. This does not mean, however, that summer and winter are therefore ideal times for meditation. But we certainly learned not to be bothered by heat or cold!

There is a couplet inscribed at the entrance to every Chinese Ch'an Hall, which says that when you enter you give up your body to the routine of the Ch'an Hall and your life to the Dharma Protector Deities. This means that you should have no concern for your body or your life. You must give yourself completely to the practice of Ch'an. Monks who went for retreat were told that if we got sick no one would care for us and if we died our bodies would be stuffed under the meditation platform and cremated after the retreat ended! This may sound harsh, but it encouraged us to let go of all our expectations and drop our attachments. Only then could we practice well.

We ate, slept, and meditated in the Ch'an Hall during retreats. Before new *bhiksus* began such an ordeal, you might think that someone would give us an orientation and tell us what was expected of us. Didn't we need to know the daily schedule and rules, not to mention the basics of how to practice? Actually, there was no explanation whatsoever. We were simply expected to do as everybody else did. In fact, if you asked how to practice you were likely to be hit with the incense board, a flat stick about three feet long used in the meditation hall to strike monks on the shoulders in order to wake them or relieve muscular tension.

Once I asked a master, "How long do we have to go through this?"

He said, "Until the year of the donkey." Unfortunately, there is no year of the donkey in the Chinese calendar. He meant that there would be no end. We were not supposed to seek explanations, which somewhat distressed me. It seemed like blind practice. But this was the method of training in the monasteries of that time. *Bhiksus* continued this "blind" practice for years, and gradually their characters and dispositions changed for the better as a result.

During retreats, there were short Dharma lectures in which practice was discussed. Interviews with the Ch'an master were not a regular feature of practice. If something unusual happened —if you had a meditative experience that seemed important, or an enlightenment experience, or a difficult problem—you could approach the head of the meditation hall. He questioned and tested you, and if you had experienced something he deemed important, he would report it to the master. The master might allow the head of the meditation hall to help you, or he might choose to see you personally. To see the master privately is called "inquiry," *xiao can* (*dokusan* in Japanese).

It was often the case that you would practice in a monastery for years without ever seeing the master privately. This was not necessarily bad. In fact it probably meant that you were practicing smoothly and doing well with the instruction given in the master's public talks, so you did not need the master to resolve questions or problems.

Today most people don't devote uninterrupted years to practice. They come to a monastery or center for short periods of time, like the seven-day retreats we have at the Ch'an Meditation Center in New York City. There are fewer participants, and it is possible for everyone to have interviews with the master. At the Ch'an Center participants have four opportunities for interview during a seven-day retreat, two with one of my assistants and two with me. If special circumstances or experiences arise unexpectedly, participants may request a special interview.

During these inquiries, the practitioner talks to the interviewer only about difficulties or questions concerning his or her present situation of the mind, body, or method of practice. He or she does not see the master or assistants to debate or discuss Buddhist teachings or even *gongan* theory, or to talk about the past or future. Such things are unnecessary. The purpose of inquiry is to seek help with the problems of the present moment.

When I was young, a monk who was given permission to enter the master's quarters to question him was recognized as a "disciple who is allowed to enter the master's room." This signified that the *bhiksu* had experienced an initial awakening or was very close to an awakening. Most *bhiksus* didn't ever get to enter the master's quarters. I never entered the master's room while I was in mainland China.

During retreat, practitioners work at basic, manual tasks such as food preparation and cleaning, and this work is also a time for practice. It offers an opportunity to train yourself for daily life, to tune your mind. Ordinarily when we work, our minds are lax and our thoughts wander. Our minds are neither at rest nor engaged in practice, and this creates tension. We practice as we work by trying to be mindful of the task at hand and where our bodies are, no matter what we are doing. We allow our minds to remain gentle and relaxed, but do not let them wander. If we can learn to do this during retreat, then we will be able to be in the midst of practice in daily life. It can be quite enjoyable!

It is because it is difficult to maintain the mind of practice in every moment and in all activities that we resort to sitting meditation. Each day we set aside time to sit and concentrate the mind, and we do this many hours a day during retreat. When we sit, we realize how scattered our minds are. As we develop more concentration and calmness through meditation, that concentration and calmness will overflow into and influence our daily lives. This is one of the purposes of sitting practice.

To return to the story of my Ch'an training; in 1949, when I was nineteen, I was a student *bhiksu* in Shanghai, and China was in turmoil with the Communist Revolution. As the Communists approached Shanghai, the only choices available to poor student *bhiksus* were to join either the Communist army or the Nationalist army. Along with other young novices, I joined the Nationalists and went to Taiwan. At that time when you enlisted in the Nationalist army, your enlistment was for life. It was over ten years before I was able to return to monastic life, and I was finally allowed to retire from the army mostly because of ill health. However, all the time I was in the army I continued to ask myself the same questions I had asked as a student *bhiksu:* "Is this all there is to practice? Am I ever going to learn more? Am I ever going to meet a liberated Ch'an master and find the solution to my problems?"

In Taiwan I practiced and asked the advice of masters when I could. I asked an eminent master, "How should I practice? What should I do?"

The master replied, "Practice! What are you talking about? What do you mean, 'practice'? This is it. Just practice what you've been doing day after day." I felt that I was going to be stuck for the rest of my life, and that I would be unable to make progress in practice. Hearing the stories of the great Ch'an patriarchs did not help my despair. For instance, Huineng, who became the Sixth Patriarch of Ch'an, began as an ordinary woodcutter. One day he heard a line from the *Diamond Sutra,* grasped it completely, and immediately attained enlightenment without any previous Buddhist practice or study! I had also heard stories of people who attained enlightenment simply by seeing, meeting, or speaking with the Buddha. Sometimes the Buddha would say just one thing to someone, such as, "Ah, you've finally come!" and that person would achieve enlightenment.

I felt that my karmic obstructions were heavy, and I despaired of ever seeing the Buddhas or encountering a liberated teacher. I had many questions and doubts, and I wondered, "I'm not stupid. Is it really possible that no one can help me understand how to practice?" No one I questioned was terribly encouraging or helpful. They would tell me, "Your karmic capacity must be poor, and you must have many karmic obstructions. Practice hard, repent, do prostrations, and venerate the Buddha."

Questions about practice would continue to plague me until I was twenty-eight. At that time I had the good fortune to meet Master Ling Yuan, a disciple and spiritual descendant of the great modern master Xuyun. I had been in the army for almost ten years, and I was doing important and exhausting administrative work. All the while, I had the "doubt sensation," a powerful, nonrational state of questioning that can result from investigating a Ch'an question. Because my health was poor, the army allowed me to take a holiday, and I chose to spend the time visiting temples in Taiwan.

As I traveled through the countryside I was able to concentrate on practice, and my doubt intensified. The beautiful scenery was invisible to me. My mind was filled with WHY? Why sit and meditate? Why not? Should I marry? Why not? The questions were of a quite ordinary nature, but I had hundreds of them, all circling the one big WHY. It didn't really matter what the specific questions were; they all joined in the doubt sensation.

At one temple the *bhiksus* treated me as a fellow *bhiksu*, even though I was in uniform. I was given a place to sleep on a traditional Chinese sleeping platform, along with another guest, Master Ling Yuan. I didn't know that this *bhiksu* was a master, but I saw how calm and peaceful the old man was. At night, Master Ling Yuan sat in meditation, so I sat next to him. After some time passed I cautiously asked him, "May I ask you a few questions?"

Master Ling Yuan said, "Fine."

I started in with my many questions, and after each one he would say, "Is that all?"

This went on for about two hours. I became puzzled and a little distressed, thinking, "He keeps asking if I have more questions but he's not answering any of them. What's going on here?" Still, I continued asking questions.

Finally, when Master Ling Yuan asked me yet again, "Any more?" I was confused, and I hesitated. Master Ling Yuan struck the platform, surprising me with the loud noise it made, and said, "Take all your questions and put them down! Who has all these questions?"

In that instant all my questions were gone. The whole world had changed. My body ran with perspiration, but felt extraordinarily light. My perspective had changed, and all at once my questions seemed laughable. The person I had been was laughable. I felt that I had dropped a thousand-pound burden. The next day the master asked, "Did you sleep well?" and I answered, "Quite well."

This was the most important experience in my life up to that point. While before I had struggled to understand the Buddhist scriptures or the records of the sayings of Ch'an masters, afterward I understood them immediately, without explanation. I felt as if they were my own words. Previously I would wonder, "What does this word mean? What is the point behind that phrase or this expression?" Now I saw that words are words and that is all. If you understand the idea behind a word, that's fine, but if you don't understand, that's fine too. People listen to my talks and ask me questions about practice and life. Some people understand what I say and some do not. Either way is fine.

The experience I had did not cause all my *duhkha*, vexations, and afflictions to simply disappear. I was still aware of them. They were no longer so evident externally, but I knew in my heart that under certain circumstances my problems would still affect me.

Duhkha can be of "principle," caused by mistaken views; or it can be "phenomenal," caused by greed, anger, and ignorance. *Duhkha* caused by incorrect views is removed by correct views. *Duhkha* caused by greed, anger, and ignorance is more basic, because greed, anger, and ignorance are beginningless. Cultivation is necessary in order to remove them. Cultivation, which removes root *duhkha*, includes observing the moral teachings of Ch'an and practicing the methods of Ch'an, such as sitting meditation, walking meditation, reciting Buddha's name, prostrations, sutra reading, and mindfulness.

What happened to me in my encounter with Master Ling Yuan was that my problems and irritations were removed. Although my perspective radically changed, my root vexations remained and would only be uprooted through cultivation. Even after you see your true nature, when afflictions occur they will still cause *duhkha*. But you will be clearly aware of them and recognize them as vexations.

Be clear about this. Do not imagine that a little bit of enlightenment will cause all your vexations to vanish. That is not the case. If a Ch'an master claims that all of his problems and vexations are gone, don't believe him! I am still an ordinary person and I still need to practice regularly. In fact, I have never seen evidence that any Ch'an patriarch or master ever claimed that he had no more vexations or that he had become a Buddha. However, even though all your vexations do not disappear with a first experience of enlightenment, your faith becomes extremely strong and is based on a firm foundation once you have glimpsed your true nature.

After my experience with Master Ling Yuan, I felt a strong need to continue to practice. With the help of several of my masters and General Cheng Kai-ming, I managed to retire from the army and become a *bhiksu* again.

I was a disciple of Master Tung-chu, a respected heir to both the Linji and Caodong lineages, and the editor of his magazine, *Humanity*. Master Tung-chu was quite a harsh teacher. He would tell me to do prostrations, and then a few days later he would say, "This is nothing but a dog eating shit. Go and read the sutras."

I would read for a couple of weeks, and then he would say, "The patriarchs thought the sutras were only good for cleaning sores. Go and write an essay."

When I wrote the essay, Master Tung-chu would tear it up, saying, "These are only stolen ideas. Use your original wisdom; say something!" He even got me to close up the door to my room and make a new door in another wall.

I was still aware of the traces of my *duhkha* internally, and knew that under certain circumstances they might manifest. As a result, I did a Great Repentance ritual that lasted thirty days.

I wanted to do a three-year solitary retreat at a small temple in southern Taiwan, but they did not have a room for me, and I did not have the funds to build the small house I would need. A Buddhist layman heard of my plight and donated the money necessary to build the retreat, and in 1961 I began what would be six years of solitary practice.

My retreat began with a simple ceremony attended by a few people, during which I was symbolically sealed into my hut. From the moment I started the retreat my mind was calm and settled, and I felt very happy, as though I had found my true home. My one meal a day was of wild potato leaves, which I grew myself. My hut had a yard, and the front looked out over a cliff. Even though I always remained in the courtyard, I never had a feeling of being closed in. Inside I had for an altar a small table I made myself, and over it a small painting of Shakyamuni Buddha. I did not have any money to buy a readymade altar or a Buddha statue. There was no running water or electricity. I drew water and bathed at a spring. After about a year, someone gave me an oil lamp as an offering, but I had no money to buy oil!

I did not concentrate on sitting meditation at first, but spent most of my time performing repentance rituals and prostrations to the Buddha. The ritual for repentance I used is called *Dabai Can*, the Great Compassionate Repentance Ceremony, and is based on the *Dharani of the Compassion of Avaloketesvara*. I also prostrated my way through the *Lotus Sutra*, doing one prostration for each of about 80,000 characters in it. This may sound like a lot of prostrations, and in fact it is. But I have heard that in Tibetan Buddhism there is a similar practice, but the practitioner does 100,000 prostrations! I guess I'm not yet up to par, as far as Tibetan tradition is concerned.

I followed this practice for about half a year. Then I began to concentrate on sitting meditation. I also read the sutras. Later in the retreat I did some writing, including two books, *The Correct Buddhist Belief* and *Essentials of Learning the Vinaya*. Originally I planned three years in retreat, but they passed so quickly that I decided to stay for three more years. However, I developed eye problems and had to interrupt my retreat for treatment. After six months I was able to return for a second three years.

When I came out of retreat, in March 1968, I felt that it was time for me to spread the Dharma. I wanted to teach people the Buddhist scriptures, teachings, and methods of practice. At that time the standard of practice was not high in Taiwan, and Buddhist *bhiksus* and *bhiksuni* were not well educated. I was particularly struck by the criticism of a Christian preacher who claimed that Buddhist *bhiksus* couldn't even read and understand the sutras. Recognizing the need for well-educated practitioners, I decided to go to Japan to study at Rissho Buddhist University. Japan has a strong tradition of Buddhist learning, and I thought I could take what I learned back to Taiwan and try to raise the quality of Buddhist education there.

In Japan I divided my time between studying and practice.

During vacations from school I went on retreat. I practiced with Rinzai, Soto Zen, and Pure Land masters at many of the major monasteries in Japan. I particularly practiced with Bantetsugu Roshi, a disciple of Harada Roshi, who had a temple in Tohoku. I did several winterlong retreats with him. He gave me *inka,* official confirmation that the student has completed training, in a combination of Rinzai and Soto Zen, and when I was leaving him he suggested that I go to America to spread Zen Buddhism.

I completed my doctoral thesis after six years, which was considered extraordinarily rapid progress. In 1975 I had returned to Taiwan, and had been there a short time when I was invited to the United States by the American Buddhist Association; I was appointed abbot of the Temple of Great Enlightenment in the Bronx, in New York City. I didn't know how I might be able to help people there, since I didn't know much about Americans and my English was rudimentary. But I came to the United States and began living at the temple, and soon people began to come to see me seeking guidance in practice.

After I had been in the United States for a while, I returned to Taiwan for a visit and went to see my two old masters. I had not received transmission from them before, because I had left to go into retreat and then to Japan, so at this time I received transmission in both lineages of Ch'an.

I said to my masters, "I am teaching Ch'an in America. Is that OK?"

They responded, "Ha, so you think you can teach Ch'an! Is that so?"

I answered, "I'm just deceiving people. Don't worry."

They said, "Oh, that's fine, then."

After that, I started teaching Ch'an in Taiwan too, deceiving people there, as well!

When I began teaching, I recalled how difficult it was for me to learn how to practice, and how long it took. No one had ever talked to me about the methods of practice and stages of development. I decided that in my own teaching I would make these things clear. Although Ch'an is not based on words and does not have techniques or stages, the Buddhist scriptures and treatises do discuss methods and stages of practice.

Work hard, work slowly, get results. This was the kind of practice I experienced in my youth. There was a conceptual basis for this method of practice, even though no one discussed it. This practice was based on the observation that with slow, hard work, eventually good results develop. If you ask people today to trust in this blind, no-method practice—a slow, deliberate process—they are unlikely to be interested. People in modern societies believe that they are too busy to spend the time this style of teaching requires, and do not understand that such practice does work. Today it is important to teach people about the methods of practice and stages of development. This gives them a foundation to work from, so that they can benefit from practice.

5

Methods of Practice and Stages of Development in Ch'an

Ch'an practice helps us to attain liberation and wisdom. We become liberated from self-centeredness and *duhkha*. With liberation comes clarity, or wisdom. All our practice and cultivation must begin with self-reflection. Our own greed, anger, ignorance, arrogance, and doubt result in *duhkha*. These are self-centered attitudes, caused by our attachment to our bodies and minds—which are a succession of ever-changing materials and thoughts. Our feelings of attachment to our bodies and minds are the result of mistaken perceptions, as are our feelings of like and dislike.

Buddhist methods of practice allow us to let go of self-centeredness and alleviate suffering. Practice also helps the concepts taught by the Buddha, including cause and effect, causes and conditions, and compassion, to take root in our lives.

The training of the mind in Ch'an practice can be divided into three levels. First, we move from a scattered state of mind to concentrated mind. Second, we move from concentrated mind to one-mind (*samadhi*). Finally, we let go of even one-mind, and reach no-mind. At that point, we have let go of our self-centeredness and realize wisdom. However, mental cultivation through practice is not enough by itself. Conduct in daily life is extremely important. Physical actions, speech, and thought constitute what Buddhists call the three kinds of actions, or the three kinds of karma. If these actions accord with Buddhist moral principles, then we are following the precepts. Contrary actions break the precepts, the Buddhist moral teachings. Act in this way and the cultivation of *samadhi* will not be successful, and wisdom will not manifest.

Scattered mind is easy to see. In this state thoughts come and go in a haphazard manner. To see what I mean, try this experiment: raise your index finger and look at it for about a minute. Just look, in a relaxed manner, and have no thoughts.

Were you able to look without thinking? If not, your mind was scattered. When we do things with a scattered mind, we are not using our fullest capacity. As you can see, achieving even concentrated mind is no easy matter.

How do we move from scattered mind to concentrated mind to one-mind and finally to no-mind? We use the methods of Ch'an.

The methods of following the breath and counting the breath were advocated by the Buddha himself in the *Sutra on the Awareness of Breathing*, and they are still commonly used to concentrate the mind. In the method of following the breath, you maintain your awareness at the tip of your nose. Do not try to direct your breath in any way. Do not pay attention to whether your breathing is long or short, or deep or shallow. Just passively be aware of the feeling of each breath as it enters your nose.

When your mind is sufficiently calm, you can use the method of counting the breath. Each time you exhale, count one number. Count from one to ten, and then start over at one. Your attention should not be on breathing itself, but on the numbers. Do not try to suppress your wandering thoughts. If you do, in the beginning it may seem as if you succeed, but as time goes on you will feel uncomfortable and more wandering thoughts will arise. Ignore the wandering thoughts and they will gradually subside by themselves. Allow your mind to relax, and each time you notice that it has wandered simply return to counting your breath. If you don't desire the pleasant, or repulse the unpleasant, your mind will naturally become focused. Ch'an practitioners should also maintain this attitude during daily life. To become annoyed with difficulties merely adds difficulty to difficulty. Maintain a mind of peace and nonopposition, and all tensions will naturally be dissolved.

If your mind is very scattered, you can make the counting more complicated by counting backward or counting only even or odd numbers. If you cannot count to ten, it doesn't matter. Don't feel disappointed. If you make mistakes in the numbers, don't feel regretful or anxious. If you are tense or anxious, then no matter what you do, using the method will seem difficult and you will not be able to use it well. No matter how many mistakes you make, maintain a joyful and relaxed attitude, and go back and start counting from one. You should feel joyful because you are aware that you have made a mistake!

Watching the breath or counting the breath is, in fact, contemplating impermanence. Breath, body movements, and numbers: all continuously change from moment to moment. Thoughts, as much as anything else, continuously arise and perish. The idea of self is generated by thoughts; or rather, from attachment to thoughts. How do we attach to thoughts? We identify with our opinions and defend them, for instance. But tomorrow our opinions and point of view will change.

When we experience the ephemeral nature of thoughts, we also experience the ephemeral nature of the self. Thoughts have no independent external existence, and neither does the self that identifies with them. The experience of impermanence is of paramount importance to one's practice. If we can directly perceive each thought as impermanent and selfless, this itself is wisdom.

Liberation from *duhkha*, suffering, comes through an understanding of the concept of impermanence followed by direct experience of this impermanence. In order to experience liberation, we must follow the moral principles of Buddhism and practice diligently. We must practice with an understanding of wisdom so that we can experience liberation directly. This is sudden enlightenment. I am not talking about worldly wisdom but *prajna*, spiritual wisdom as it is understood in Buddhism. A person who has realized wisdom is not driven by desire and aversion. Instead, he responds naturally to whatever happens, in order to help other sentient beings experience wisdom.

Every method of practice can bring you to profound levels of clarity. While you are counting your breath, your concentration can become deeper and deeper until there seem to be no numbers for you to count and no breathing. If this state of mind is clear and sustained, then it is an elementary level of one mind, the stage after scattered mind. You and your method of practice become one. Body and mind are no longer separate but are fused or absorbed into a single stream of concentration. You may feel that your body has lost its weight or heaviness and disappeared. What you really experience is a fully unified and integrated body and mind, and a concentrated mind.

At the intermediate level of one-mind you feel that whatever your senses encounter, what you see and hear, is the same as yourself. The sense organs no longer have separate functions, and there is no distinction between what you see and what you hear. Next, this unified mind can deepen and become more refined until you feel that there is no distinction between inside and outside or between yourself and environment. It feels as though the one and the two are absolutely unified in oneness.

Then the distinction or division between thoughts disappears. There is a steady single point of concentration, or stream of concentration. A single thought, if you will. This is a deeper level of one-mind.

If that one thought disappears, one-mind also disappears, and you experience no-mind: you see your intrinsic nature. When that one thought disappears, the self-attachment that perpetuates the thought also disappears. This last stage—the exploding and disappearance of the single concentrated stream of thought, one-mind, into no-thought or no-mind—is not only the aim of Ch'an, it is the method and practice of Ch'an as well.

There are other meditation practices that are similar to counting the breath. For instance, the Chinese often recite the name of Amitabha Buddha as a method of concentrating the mind. This works in the same way as counting the breath, and it too may be practiced until a one-mind or even a no-mind state is reached.

Another common method is *shikantaza*. This method was derived from the silent illumination method used by the Cao-dong sect of Ch'an (in Japanese, *Soto*) by the Japanese master Dogen (1200–1253). Dogen received Dharma transmission from the Chinese Caodong master Rujing (1163–1228).

Shikantaza literally means "just minding sitting." You maintain awareness of your whole body while you sit in meditation. The important thing is to be mindful of the whole body, not part of the body. Even when you have sensations in parts of your body, such as pain, itchiness, cold, or even pleasant sensations, maintain awareness of your whole body. When you can do this, sensations in parts of your body will not bother you much. After all, they are only a small part of what you are aware of.

As your wandering thoughts are extinguished, your awareness that your body is sitting erect and present will become very clear. Who is sitting? It is you. Do not watch yourself as if you are watching somebody else. As your practice of *shikantaza* deepens, your body and the environment merge so that you no longer perceive them as separate, and your mind unifies into one-mind. If you continue to practice *shikantaza* you can go on to realize the deeper states of meditation.

Practitioners may continue to use counting the breath, reciting Buddha's name, or *shikantaza* indefinitely. However, in Ch'an practice, after the one-mind state has been reached we often use the methods of *hua to, gongan,* or silent illumination to break apart one-mind and realize no-mind.

A *hua to* is a question that you "investigate" (*can*). *Hua* means "word," *to* means "head" or "source." When we practice using a *hua to,* we want to know, "What is there?" before the application of any literal or symbolic description (*hua*). Dahui Zong-gao (1089–1163) was the great advocate of the *hua to* method. Examples of *hua to* we use today are "Who am I?," "What is *wu?*" (*wu* means "no" or "nothing"), "Who is reciting the Buddha's name?," and "Who is dragging this corpse around?"

At the first level of *hua to* practice you simply repeat the *hua to*. In this way you develop concentration, as you do in the first level of counting the breath or reciting a Buddha's name. Even to be able to do this well is good. The next level is asking or querying the *hua to*. At this level the special quality of the *hua to* method begins to be evident. Eventually your questioning begins to have some meaning, and you begin to truly desire to penetrate the *hua to*. Then you are ready to *"can,"* or "investigate" the *hua to*.

When you are deeply engaged with the investigation of the *hua to*, the doubt sensation arises. You truly want to know the answer to this question, and you become so tied up with it that it's not easy for you to be interrupted. You are like a hungry child with a piece of candy. You cannot be distracted and will not let go.

One day, when I was in the mountains practicing, I walked down the steps from the hut where I was living and my mind suddenly filled with doubt. I thought, "Who just walked down the steps? It was me. But who is standing here now? It is also me. Then is the me who just walked downstairs a moment ago the same as the me who is down here now, or am I two different people?" I became so wrapped up in that question that I didn't eat that day.

In that case the doubt sensation arose spontaneously. There is a lot of power in that kind of natural doubt. However, most people do not give rise to doubt spontaneously, so they use a method, such as investigating the *hua to* "Who am I?" to help bring it out. If you are practicing hard, such a question can have great significance.

During a retreat in Taiwan, I saw that a student was ripe. I asked him, "What is your name?"

He replied, "Ch'en . . ."

I said, "That's wrong. Ch'en . . . is over there!" and I pointed to the name card pasted on the wall above his cushion.

He said, "What am I doing over there?"

He couldn't figure out who he was. For over twenty years he had considered his name to be himself. But now he realized his name had nothing to do with him. So who was he? The doubt sensation arose in his mind. The sensation of doubt is like being in a pitch-black room, or inside an iron ball. You cannot see anything at all, but you know there must be some brightness outside and you really want to know what it is.

If the *hua to* method seems to you like chewing cotton, completely tasteless, then you are still at the level of repeating the *hua to*. If you are easily interrupted or distracted in your practice, then you are also at the first level. By the time you begin to sincerely ask the *hua to,* you already have a genuine desire to penetrate the question. The desire to penetrate the question cannot be simulated. You must develop good concentration and genuinely apply the method. You also cannot use your intellect to think about the question and come up with an answer. That will not produce or break apart the one-mind state.

As your investigation of the *hua to* becomes more and more powerful, your doubt becomes "great doubt." At this point you are no longer aware of your body, of the world, or of anything else. Only the questioning, the great doubt, is left. Once again, this is one-mind.

It is very important to distinguish whether a practitioner has entered into the "condition" in which the great doubt sensation has been generated. Before the generation of great doubt, the master may allow an exhausted practitioner to take a rest, the length of which depends upon the degree of her exhaustion. However, after entering into the condition of great doubt, the master will drive the practitioner like someone driving a herd of wild animals. There can be no stopping. If a person is healthy, when she has generated great doubt no harm can come to her body, no matter how strenuously she practices. This is because at this stage she is in complete harmony with the universe, and the power of the universe is available to her. The master must push the practitioner to keep going and going and going, in the hope that a world-shattering explosion will take place, that one-mind will break apart and no-mind be revealed.

A *hua to* is a phrase, a sentence, or a question whose meaning you want to grasp at its source. A *gongan*, or koan, in contrast, is the story of a complete event, and you investigate the whole incident in order to grasp what it is about, even if it seems bizarre and incomprehensible. *Gongan* means "public case."

The story of Master Nanchuan Puyuan (in Japan, Nansen Fugan, 748–835) and the cat is a *gongan*.[11] Two groups of monks in a monastery were disputing the ownership of a cat. The abbot, Master Nanchuan, came back to the monastery and witnessed the dispute. He grabbed the cat and said, "Say one thing," meaning something demonstrating a realization of Ch'an, "and you can save this cat."

Nobody dared to say anything, so Nanchuan cut the cat in

11. Cleary and Cleary, *The Blue Cliff Record*, Cases 63 and 64, pp. 358 and 361.

two. Later an accomplished disciple, Zhaozhou (Joshu, 788–897), returned to the monastery. When Nanchuan told him the story, he took off his shoe, put it on his head, and left the room.

Nanchuan remarked, "If he had been here earlier, the cat wouldn't have died."

To practice using this *gongan* is to ask, "What is this story all about?" However, practitioners often misunderstand how to use a *gongan*. When a *gongan* happens, it is a living event, but after that it is dead and you cannot follow the outline, the sequence of events, and think that it will precipitate a change in you. Impossible! If you ask me questions for hours, like I did when I questioned Master Ling Yuan, and then I bang my fist down and say, "Put your questions down!" like he did, do you think you will see your intrinsic nature?

Each person has his or her own circumstances, or causes and conditions, and when the causes and conditions mature properly, then something like what happened to me can happen. This does not mean that you can expect causes and conditions to mature by themselves. It requires practice.

It is not unusual for people to read *gongan* and other stories about Ch'an masters and then try to act them out, seeking an identical outcome for themselves. For example, someone might want to emulate the encounter between Master Dayu and Linji. Linji was a disciple of Huangbo, who hit him whenever he tried to ask a question. Later Linji studied with Dayu. Dayu said something which made him see that Huangbo had been kind to him, and he realized enlightenment.

Someone who attended Ch'an retreats had read such stories,

and when I hit him with the incense board he grabbed it and tried to hit me back. I grabbed the board and said, "So, you think you are enlightened!"

He responded, "Ah, you see that I'm enlightened!"

I replied, "You are not enlightened, so don't hit me."

You cannot realize enlightenment by imitating others, but you can become enlightened through virtually any activity. You can become enlightened by plugging in your TV, walking your dog, or being hit. It depends upon your spiritual maturity and readiness. Then anything can be a catalyst. How do we become ready? By behaving according to the precepts (right action), having a correct understanding of the Buddhadharma (right view), and by using the methods of Ch'an (right concentration).

In the Ming Dynasty, Master Hanshan taught his disciples to practice by using one word: *she*, "let go," which is a kind of *hua to*. Master Hanshan lived from 1546 to 1623. He began as a practitioner of Pure Land Buddhism, and followed the Pure Land practice of reciting Buddha's name. When he was twenty someone taught him the Ch'an *hua to* "Who is reciting Buddha's name?" At twenty-eight he settled on Hanshan mountain and took its name, as the Buddhist poet Hanshan had taken it before him. At thirty-one he reached a deep state of *samadhi*, or meditative concentration. Afterward he read the *Surangama Sutra* and "completed his understanding." At forty he had another profound awakening.

How did Master Hanshan teach? What does it mean to "let go"? Whenever a thought arises, drop it immediately. To drop it doesn't mean to resist it or to try to throw it away. Your mind must be relaxed, and you ignore the thoughts. While you are paying attention to your method it is common for stray thoughts to appear, especially in the beginning. Don't let them disturb you. Just ignore the thoughts and attend to your method. If you don't seem to be getting anywhere in your meditation practice, you are probably unable to let go.

Problems with stray thoughts fall into two categories: first, you notice the thought but can't make it go away; the more you try to chase it away, the more thoughts come up. Or you don't notice the thoughts at first—the second category of problem— and when you finally discover that your thoughts have strayed, you have gone off the track in a whole train of wandering thoughts.

The first type of problem is like being surrounded by flies while eating something sweet. If you wave your arms about, the flies will just disperse and swarm back again. The best way to deal with this problem is not to bother with the flies. As soon as you've eaten the food, the flies will naturally disappear. If you attend to your method and don't try to push thoughts away, they will eventually disappear.

The second type of problem is similar to dozing off while riding a horse, so that you are not aware when he leaves the path and starts wandering around eating grass. When you finally do realize it, minutes may have passed. Don't get upset when you realize that your thoughts have wandered. Anxiety will just cause more thoughts to arise. Instead of regretting the past, relax your mind and go back to your method.

There are many levels to the practice of letting go. The first step is to let go of the past and future and just concentrate on the present. This sounds easy, but it is not. All stray thoughts are connected with the past or the future. The second step is to let go of the present moment, which consists of two parts—the "outside," or the environment, and the "inside," which can be further divided into the body and the mind. First we must let go of the environment, because thoughts come about through the contact of our physical senses with the environment. Temperature, cars, birds, the wind, the sounds people make, light or darkness, etc., all influence us to give rise to thoughts. Since it is impossible to meditate in a place where absolutely nothing will disturb you from outside, the only way to deal with the environment is to let go. Until you reach the point of concentrating only on your mind and body, and not on the environment, you will experience sensations from outside. But instead of letting them annoy you, drop them when they arise.

After letting go of the environment, the third step is to let go of yourself. First, let go of your body. Long ago there was a great Ch'an practitioner who always fell asleep while meditating. In order to combat the problem, he placed his meditation seat on top of a rock at the edge of a cliff. He knew that if he dozed off, he would fall to his death. A person like this will practice very well because he no longer cares about his body. He is prepared to die if he does not practice well. If you worry about your body, if you are aware of uncomfortable, or even pleasurable, sensations, then you will never enter a good state of concentration.

Many people imagine that it is easier to let go of the body

than to let go of the environment. Actually, it is extremely difficult not to pay attention to your body. However, if you attend single-mindedly to your method, eventually you will forget the existence even of your body, and only your concentration will remain. At this point concentrated mind has deepened into one-mind.

There are two other things I should discuss along with *hua to* and *gongan,* although they are used in other situations as well: *ji-feng* (the "right opportunity" for Ch'an) and *zhuan-yu* ("turning words"). In general, *ji-feng* fall into two types. Sometimes a person is practicing and working very well, yet he cannot emerge into a new state. At this point, the master may give him a spontaneous, direct, sudden action to trigger a change. For example, the practitioner is very thirsty and the master gives him a glass of water. Just as he reaches for the glass to drink, the master grabs the glass and smashes it on the floor, and asks, "Do you still need a drink of water?" Such an incident may help tremendously. This is the first type of *ji-feng.*

The second type of *ji-feng* is a particular kind of dialogue between accomplished Ch'an masters. The inner meaning is abstruse, while the words may sound meaningless or self-contradictory. For example, one master might say, "It is raining in the eastern mountains, the western mountains become wet." Another master may answer, "A mud ox entered the sea and nothing has been heard of him since." Such words, when recorded, sometimes become *gongans.*

Zhuan-yu means "turning words." *Zhuan-yu* turn around a practitioner's conceptions and attitudes. An example is in the *gongan* of Master Baizhang (in Japanese, Hyakujo, 720–814) and the fox.[12] Once, while Master Baizhang was lecturing, an old man with white hair and white beard was sitting in the audience. At the end of the lecture, he approached Baizhang and said, "Master, please give me a *zhuan-yu*. Five hundred lifetimes ago, I was already a *bhiksu*. At that time I told someone that an enlightened being is not subject to cause and consequence. Ever since then I have been reborn as a fox, lifetime after lifetime. Is there something you can say to me which will help me to leave the life of a fox?"

Baizhang said, "Instead of saying 'not subject to cause and consequence,' you should say, 'cause and consequence never fail.'"

Hearing this, the old man was very happy and bowed three times and left. Later that day Baizhang and his disciples found the corpse of a fox, and they gave him the funeral of a *bhiksu*.

This *gongan* illustrates how a few words can "turn around" ideas to which we are deeply attached, and bring great benefits.

When Gaofeng Yuanmiao (*Koho Gemmyo*, 1238–1295) had already been working on the *hua to* "What is *wu*?" for a long time, he met Master Xueyan Zuching (Seggan Sokin, 1216–1287). The master said to him, "You have been practicing for so long. At this point, can you be your own master during the

---

12. Aitken, *The Gateless Barrier*, Case 2, p. 19.

daytime?" He was asking if Gaofeng had control over his thoughts and actions, so that he did not think about what he did not want to think about, and did not do what he did not want to do.

Gaofeng immediately replied, "Yes, I can!"

Xueyan asked, "At night in your dreams, can you be your own master?"

Gaofeng answered promptly, "Yes, I can."

Xueyan asked, "When you are sleeping without any dreams, where is the master then?"

Despite all his practice, Gaofeng was stumped. He repeated the question to himself but could not give an answer. So Xueyan told Gaofeng, "From now on, do not study the Buddhadharma, and do not read the sutras and sastras. Just practice well. How should you practice? When you are hungry, eat. When you are tired, go to sleep. When you have slept enough, get up and practice."

From that time onward, Gaofeng heeded Xueyan's words. When he was hungry, he ate; when he was tired, he slept; and he tried very hard to practice. What did he practice? He asked himself the *hua to* "Where is my master?" He used this method for five years. Even during sleep he asked himself, "Who am I?" because this question caused him to generate great doubt. We should remember that even before he started on this *hua to*, he had already reached the state where he could be his own master in the daytime and in his dreams. His concentration was very powerful.

One night he awoke from sleep and reached out to feel for

his pillow. The pillow dropped from the sleeping platform with a thud. At the sound, the cloud of doubt was broken, and one-mind dropped away. Gaofeng shouted, "A-ha, now I found you!" He felt he had emerged from inside a pitch-black barrel to see the light!

In *hua to* and *gongan* practice, the transition from one-mind to no-mind is catalyzed by great doubt. However, there are other kinds of practice that catalyze this change in other ways. One is silent illumination.

Silent illumination, or *mo chao,* is the most direct method of practice, because Ch'an is not something that you can think about or use words or language to describe. Its greatest advocate was the Sung Dynasty master Hongzhi Zhengjue (1091–1157), but its use can be traced back at least as far as Bodhidharma. It is the mainstay of Caodong Ch'an practice. As a matter of fact, from the point of view of the Caodong sect, every beginner should use this method.

The method of silent illumination is simply to do away with all methods of practice. Using no method is the method. Counting breath is used when the mind is very scattered in order to concentrate the mind. The methods of *hua to* and *gongan* are used when your mind is calm, but that doesn't mean that you don't have any thoughts. These methods are used to engage yourself with a question until you don't have any other thoughts left. But when you use silent illumination, your mind simply doesn't have any thoughts. You let go of everything and realized the state of Ch'an itself.

"Silent" doesn't mean that your mind is blank or asleep. It

does not even mean that there is no sound! It means no
thoughts: the mind is not moving. "Illumination," or "bright
openness," means that your mind is clear. In "illumination" you
may not be aware of the environment, space, and time, but you
are aware and clear about your own mental state. This awareness is pure consciousness. It is not a thought.

I have described many methods practitioners can use to concentrate the mind and develop wisdom during sitting meditation,
but these are not the only methods of Ch'an. Compassionate
contemplation is a method that helps eliminate anger and gives
rise to compassion for sentient beings. It is unlike the methods
of practice in which you concentrate your mind on, for instance,
numbers, breathing, or the body. Instead, it uses abstract contemplation.

The practice of compassionate contemplation involves realizing the suffering of sentient beings and seeking to help them
alleviate this suffering. One strives to bring happiness to sentient
beings, by either helping with their daily lives or helping them
to realize enlightenment. Someone who is practicing this contemplation with a Bodhi-mind would seek to help others to free
themselves from suffering in the physical and psychological
realms, and, if causes and conditions are correct, to derive happiness from the Dharma.

We have compassion, in Buddhism, for sentient beings. Remember that Buddhism traditionally differentiates between sentient beings, including animals and people, which experience

suffering, and plants, which Buddhists traditionally believe do not experience pain and suffering. Buddhists believe that all sentient beings have Buddha nature, and can realize Buddhahood eventually.

There are five stages of compassionate contemplation. The first is called "contemplation of sentient beings." This is done by observing how we generally divide sentient beings into three groups: those who are beneficial to us, those who are harmful to us, and those who are neither beneficial nor harmful. If you think about it, you will probably notice that this is part of the way you see others. For instance, a friend who drives you to the airport seems beneficial, a boss who won't let you take vacation when you want seems harmful, and the person who is behind you in line at the supermarket seems neither beneficial nor harmful.

The second stage of compassionate contemplation is to contemplate oneself. When we interact with sentient beings we generally experience two types of feelings and perceptions: like and dislike. Why do we have these feelings? They are based upon the perceived beneficial or harmful effect the present interaction will have on our bodies and minds. It is because we are attached to our bodies and minds that we have feelings of like and dislike. But we should remember that our bodies and minds are impermanent. They are merely an unending succession of ever-changing materials and thoughts. The way we conceive of our bodies and minds is the result of false perceptions, and illusions. We act as if we are permanent and unchanging, and the center of the universe, but how many centers of the universe can there be?

We each act as if we are independent and own our "self," but how long could we exist without the support of others? If we let go of our false perceptions, there is no need to be attached to our bodies and minds, and no reason to feel like or dislike in our interactions with others. For instance, if we recognize that our opinions are impermanent and constantly changing, there is no reason to be attached to them, and there is no reason to dislike someone who disagrees with us. The feelings of attachment, like, and dislike are all based upon erroneous ideas about our bodies and minds.

The third stage of compassionate contemplation involves a closer investigation of what really happens in our interactions with others. We contemplate all interactions as the physical contact of one body with another. Praise or rebuke are only vibrations entering our ears. The actions of others, such as a smile or frown, are only light rays perceived by our eyes. Just as the body is an illusion, so are these external, material phenomena also unreal. Once we realize this, we no longer need to give rise to feelings of like or dislike based on what we hear or see, and we can treat all sentient beings as equal. But at this point we still have not given rise to true compassion. How is it possible to have compassion toward unreal external sensations and illusory beings who are related only to our own illusory bodies and minds?

The fourth stage of the practice of compassionate contemplation again involves the contemplation of sentient beings. However, this time the contemplation focuses on their suffering. We suffer because we are ignorant. We don't know why we do things. We may be happy or angry, but we do not know why we are subject to these moods. We are attached to many things, like our status, possessions, family, health, and intelligence, and we are fearful of losing them. So we suffer.

In addition, sentient beings are not free in body and mind, and this causes suffering. There are things we know we should do, but we don't do them, like giving and being generous. There are things we don't want to do, but we do them anyway, like getting angry over petty annoyances. Sometimes it is as if there are two selves inside, struggling toward different ends!

We also suffer because we are born, grow old, and die. In the very short span of our lives, each of us has to endure all kinds of suffering and affliction of the body and mind, such as sickness and loss of loved ones. Even the very natural growing up and leaving home of children can cause suffering. Because of the suffering all of us undergo, we should have compassion for all sentient beings.

The fifth stage of compassionate contemplation also entails contemplating others, but now we view them all as equal; combining the three groups of those who are beneficial, harmful, or neutral to us. How is this done? It happens when we realize that our relationships with others are not fixed and unchanging. In terms of the three times—past, present, and future—we cannot say that those with whom we are close in the present were not our enemies at some time in the past, or vice versa. There is no definite, unchanging relationship of closeness or adversity. Seen from the perspective of the three times, all sentient beings have had some interaction with us in the past and will probably have some interaction with us in the future. From this point of view, we can see all beings as equal and can feel compassion for them. By practicing these stages of compassionate contemplation, we diminish our self-centeredness and allow our compassion to develop.

Doing prostrations is another Ch'an practice that can help us generate compassion. We may prostrate to express repentance, to recognize our shortcomings and the harm we have caused to sentient beings in the past, to show gratitude to the Three Jewels (Buddha, Dharma, and Sangha), to develop concentration; or we may do formless prostrations.

Repentance prostrations require a sense of shame and humility. I always have trouble communicating this point because there is no English word that fully conveys the meaning of the Chinese character. "Shame" and "humility" both have connotations that are different from the Chinese, but they are the best that we can do. If I describe it, perhaps you will get the correct idea. In order to give rise to humility, you must develop the capacity for introspection. Introspection, or self-reflection, is directed toward body (action), speech (verbal action), and mind (thought), the three elements that create karma. Introspection, if conducted honestly, will naturally lead to the realization that most of our behavior is self-centered, and causes *duhkha* for ourselves and others. Without introspection we rarely recognize our own faults. We often blame others or the environment, and see ourselves as victims. With recognition of our self-centeredness will come a better understanding of our motivations, and of our misinterpretation and misunderstanding of those motivations. This will help us gradually cease doing harm to others. A sense of shame and humility, and the motivation to change our behavior, arise from these insights into our ignorant self-centeredness.

Shakyamuni Buddha himself told his disciples that developing a sense of shame and humility was a fundamental part of practice. A person without these qualities is incomplete and cannot sincerely repent or alleviate karmic obstructions to practice. It will be difficult for him to benefit from practice and a teacher's guidance.

Karmic obstructions can stifle progress in many ways. Karmic obstructions are those same self-centered attitudes: greed, hatred, ignorance, arrogance, and doubt.

Karmic obstructions can impede your ability to find and work with a good teacher. Don't think that teachers are omniscient. You must take the initiative to ask the teacher for help and guidance. Your inability to seek or accept advice is due to your karmic obstructions. They may manifest in your character, expressions, ideas, or actions. Each can act as a wall separating you from your teacher. Your wall makes you invisible or unrecognizable. It does not allow the teacher to offer help.

If you can generate humility and a sense of shame, and sincerely repent your self-centered actions, you will develop a receptive mind. With a receptive mind you will meet good teachers and be helped by them. With a humble and receptive manner, your karmic obstructions will lighten. When our concept of self changes, our ability to receive help will increase. Humility and shame will enable you to repent and be open to a more harmonious and peaceful existence. You'll no longer waste energy in an attempt to protect yourself and reject others. When all self-centeredness ceases, genuine and full compassion can manifest.

To help us develop humility and a sense of shame, we practice repentance prostrations. As you prostrate, first remember your childhood. Try to remember all the things you said and did that hurt others. Do the same for your teenage years, early adulthood, and so on up to the present. It is necessary, while doing repentance prostrations, to look deeply into your heart.

Because we don't know how to resolve the conflicts that arise from introspection, and don't know how to deal with the emotional turmoil that results from such memories, we often avoid self-reflection. However, when you do prostrations it is the time to recognize shortcomings and repent. Afterward, you will be purged of negative emotions and have a pure mind again. Then you should vow not to repeat your mistakes.

The Dharma of Ch'an is introspection. Through introspection we gain a clear understanding of our strengths and weaknesses. With intimate knowledge of ourselves comes greater faith in ourselves. This faith will enable us to interact with others and the world with more tolerance and harmony. To cultivate Ch'an is to transform ourselves, not the environment. Once we are transformed, the environment will also, quite naturally, have transformed, and we can positively influence everyone we come in contact with.

If you maintain a mind of humility, then you can practice

any time, any place. Also, every situation you encounter and every person you meet can be both a source and a recipient of help. It depends on your point of view.

Important Ch'an practices are described in *Two Entries and Four Practices*, attributed to Bodhidharma. Bodhidharma was an Indian Buddhist monk who brought *dhyana* meditation teachings to China in about 475 A.D. He was also the First Patriarch of Chinese Ch'an.

"Four practices" refers to four different methods leading to the realization of Ch'an. The fourth and most advanced of these is "the practice of union with the Dharma." Remember that "dharma" means "all phenomena"; it is a basic tenet of Buddhism that all phenomena are impermanent and do not have an intrinsic self. In the practice of union with the Dharma we try to personally experience this impermanence and selflessness through direct contemplation of emptiness.

This is the highest practice of Ch'an and leads to the highest attainment. But it is not easy and can be discouraging. Unless we can make use of the practice of union with the Dharma without becoming discouraged or tense, we should start with more fundamental practices.

Entry through principle is similar to the practice of union with the Dharma. "Principle," like "dharma," means "all phenomena." People often think of specific phenomena, including events, objects, beings, time, etc., as separate from some sort of substratum or basic substance. But phenomena and the substance of phenomena are not separate; principle is not separate from phenomena or Dharma. When a person has no more self-centeredness or self-attachment, and sees his or her intrinsic nature, everything in the phenomenal world continues to exist except self-centeredness and self-attachment. This is entry through principle. In this state our minds are not blank. But we do not enter this state through the thinking process.

According to legend, Bodhidharma meditated for nine years facing a wall in a cave on Mt. Sung in China. The method he recommended to accomplish entry through principle is, "Make your mind like a wall." But what does this mean? We can use a wall for all sorts of things: for privacy, to hang things on, to put windows in, and so on, but the wall remains, unmoving. If your mind is like a wall, it also doesn't move. People around you may express their personalities, emotions, behaviors, and so on, but these do not give rise to self-centered responses in your mind. You are alert and respond to the environment in an unself-centered way, providing help for those around you. This is compassion.

The second "entry" is through practice. "Practice" refers to the gradual training of the mind, and Bodhidharma discusses four specific methods: accepting karmic retribution, adapting to favorable conditions, no-seeking, and union with the Dharma. Each practice is progressively more advanced, and so should be used in sequence. The fourth, union with the Dharma, we have already discussed.

Accepting karmic retribution requires recognizing the effects of karma, or causes and consequence, and accepting responsibility for what happens to us. Remember that "cause and consequence" is a special Buddhist concept and means that every action (cause) has a result (consequence), which then becomes the cause for another consequence, and so on. The chain of actions (karma) rolls along as a result of cause and consequence. When we face adversity or good fortune we should understand that we are receiving karmic retribution from previous actions in countless previous lives. If we have this perspective when misfortunes arise, we will be tranquil and without resentment. We will not suffer from disturbing emotions or be discouraged or depressed. So this is an important practice.

When I feel warm I take off my sweater. Why don't I accept feeling warm and uncomfortable as retribution for my previous karma?

"Cause and consequence" has to be understood and applied in conjunction with another Buddhist concept, "cause and conditions." "Cause and conditions" describes the fact that things happen because of many conditions coming together. We cannot and should not run away from our responsibilities and the retribution caused by our karma. But we should try to improve our conditions and karma if we can.

The second of the four practices recommended by Bodhidharma is "adapting to favorable conditions." It also requires an understanding of "cause and conditions." Adapting to conditions means that we should do our best within the limits of the constraints of our environment. If our circumstances are fortunate or something good happens to us, we should not be overly excited, because good fortune, like bad, is a result of karmic retribution. The practice of adapting to favorable conditions means that we accept our karma or "cause and consequence" without being overly joyful or self-satisfied.

Accepting karmic retribution and adapting to favorable conditions are helpful practices in daily life. They allow us to improve our conditions and karma, and maintain a positive attitude. They help us to enjoy equanimity in the face of changing circumstances, improve our behavior, and maintain harmonious relationships. These teachings of Bodhidharma are not hard to understand, and anyone can make use of them. If we can apply them in daily circumstances, we will not avoid our responsibilities, and we will make the best of our opportunities.

The third of Bodhidharma's four practices is the practice of "no-seeking." This is much more difficult than the first two practices. There is a Chinese saying that people "raise children to help them in old age, and accumulate food in case of famine." Today people in the West may not raise children just to support them in old age, but people probably still accumulate wealth in case of hard times. People certainly save money in order to use it later. This attitude is not the attitude of no-seeking. In the practice of no-seeking, you diligently engage in useful activity, yet have no thought that this activity is for your personal gain now or in the future. You do not look for any personal benefit. This is not easy, and it is a higher level of practice than the first two.

In Buddhist practice we have to leave behind our selves and our personal history, and experience selflessness before we can be enlightened. If your sense of self is strong, solid, and formidable, then there is no way you can experience enlightenment. If you are attached to the idea of attaining enlightenment or Buddhahood, you cannot succeed. Attachment to your self or to attainment is in complete contradiction to the fundamental spirit of Ch'an Buddhism. Remember that two of the principles of Ch'an are that all phenomena are impermanent, and that they have no self. If a person is attached to his own attainment, he cannot possibly be in accord with impermanence and selflessness, and therefore cannot be enlightened. Even if she has an experience or breakthrough during meditation, it is not yet Ch'an enlightenment.

Now you may feel a little disappointed. You may think, "If I should not desire enlightenment, why am I learning about Buddhism?" In Buddhism it is important to make vows and arouse the Bodhi-mind. Vows are discussed in the *Platform Sutra* of Huineng. There are four great vows: to help all sentient beings, to terminate all vexations, to learn all Buddhadharma, and to attain the highest enlightenment, or Buddhahood. The goal of enlightenment is included in our most important vows. How can we understand this in relationship to the practice of no-seeking?

When we practice the first two of Bodhidharma's four practices, accepting karmic retribution and adapting to favorable conditions, the rule of cause and consequence for our own selves is very important to us. It is normal for people to begin to learn and practice Buddhism for their own benefit. They would like to attain Buddhahood. Eventually, through practice, their self-centeredness and selfishness begin to fall away, and they no longer think so much about themselves. They find themselves busy because people need their help, and they provide what is needed, just like the wall we talked about before. They become compassionate and thus no longer think about attaining enlightenment.

You must cease to be concerned about your own attainment in order to realize enlightenment. Otherwise you will have subtle wandering thoughts and attachment to the desire to do something about yourself. If you want to free yourself from *duhkha*, and you desire liberation, you are still attached to your self. It is only when you have no concern about your own enlightenment that you can truly be enlightened. The practice of no-seeking is the practice of this enlightened state.

In the *Platform Sutra* it is said that even after a person is enlightened, he should continue to make the four great vows: to help sentient beings, to terminate vexations, to learn Buddha-dharma, and to attain Buddhahood. The difference is that after enlightenment you do not perceive anything as separate from your own self-nature. There are no sentient beings other than self-nature, no vexations other than self-nature, no Dharma other than self-nature, and no Buddhahood other than self-nature; and, of course, self-nature is empty. You continue to function, helping sentient beings, terminating vexations, and learning the Dharma, with an unmoving, natural, spontaneous mind. There will be no specific thought or goal to seek. Buddhahood is realized in this state of mind.

6.

Enlightenment? But What Is It?

You have probably heard of enlightenment, but are you clear about what it is and what it takes to attain it? Sometimes people believe that achieving enlightenment is a short and simple process! They are misled by Ch'an stories and koans in which practitioners attain enlightenment after a single word or deed, and don't realize that the practitioner involved usually meditated and studied for many years. Such uninformed people think they can become enlightened by reading a book or two. The term "sudden enlightenment" can be especially misleading. People hear this and think enlightenment requires little, if any, practice. They wait for enlightenment to strike them spontaneously. It is true that the Ch'an sect advocates going directly to the third stage of the Bodhisattva Path, which means to realize complete enlightenment immediately, but few can do this.

What does it take to generate wisdom and attain enlightenment? You must learn to put aside self-centeredness. As self-centeredness lessens, so does *duhkha*, and wisdom begins to manifest. This is not yet enlightenment, but it is already beneficial to yourself and others. Generating Bodhi-mind, the aspiration to selfless action for the sake of sentient beings, is the way to let go of self-centeredness.

Bodhi-mind is easily summarized by the four vows we chant during morning and evening services and before meals:

> *I vow to deliver innumerable sentient beings.*
> *I vow to cut off endless vexations.*
> *I vow to master limitless approaches to Dharma.*
> *I vow to attain supreme Buddhahood.*

Notice that the first vow says nothing about enlightenment. Enlightenment comes last. The first vow is to deliver sentient beings. This means that you put the welfare of sentient beings before your own welfare in all of your actions, words, and thoughts. If the good of others is in your thoughts, words, and actions, then you have generated Bodhi-mind.

Most of the time, people think first of themselves. This is the normal condition for sentient beings, but it is not Bodhi-mind. When you are serving only yourself, what you gain is limited, but if your actions are selfless, what you gain is much more expansive. Remember, you too are a sentient being. When you act to help sentient beings, you automatically help yourself. And in helping others in a selfless manner, you also gain the minds and hearts of others. Other sentient beings will follow and support you in your efforts. In this manner you are on the path to realizing yourself as a bodhisattva.

When your thoughts and actions are directed toward helping others, the second vow—to cut off, or let go of, your vexations—naturally occurs, because you will be less self-centered. The third vow—to master the approaches to the Dharma, the myriad methods and teachings of the Buddha—allows you to use the Dharma to help others. As you listen to advanced practitioners' advice and study the sutras in order to develop "right view," and use the methods of practice to develop wisdom and compassion, you will see more clearly how to help sentient beings and cut off *duhkha*.

The fourth vow is to attain Buddhahood, but you shouldn't think that Buddhahood is a goal to be sought after. Rather, Buddhahood, which is complete compassion and wisdom, is the natural culmination and manifestation of delivering sentient beings, cutting off vexations, and mastering Buddhadharma.

Your reasons for practicing the Buddha Path should be to deliver sentient beings and to cut off vexations. Do not seek anything, but generate Bodhi-mind for the sake of Bodhi-mind. The process itself is the goal, and Bodhi-mind will naturally manifest as your self-centeredness lessens. In doing this you are already delivering sentient beings. Everyone you encounter will benefit from your presence because your actions are not based on selfishness. This is compassion.

It's impossible to achieve Buddhist enlightenment without first generating Bodhi-mind. You may have profound experiences on retreat, and that is good. If they serve to generate Bodhi-mind, that is excellent. Such experiences usually leave you feeling relaxed, free, light, and stable, and they increase your faith. But if you take such experiences to be enlightenment or profound accomplishment, then you are mistaken. This very belief in your own enlightenment is self-centered and sets you apart, in your own mind, from other sentient beings, thus betraying your attachment to illusion. The four characteristics that create the sense of self—ego, personality, being, and life—are still present, and therefore the self still has a solid, firm existence. This is why, from the Ch'an point of view, the person who believes in his own enlightenment is not really completely enlightened. If the belief that your experiences indicate saintly levels of Buddhist accomplishment persists, we consider it a form of delusion called "Ch'an sickness," or a "demonic state." Such feelings are an obstruction to practice.

Suppose that after much practice you experience the feeling of disappearance of the self into enlightenment. Tremendous bliss wells up in you, and you think, "Truly, my self has disappeared completely and I have entered enlightenment." Have you really entered enlightenment, though? Since you still approach enlightenment with a sense of self, the final achievement is still unrealized. However, experiences like this are so powerful that they are likely to mislead even an experienced practitioner.

Once, during retreat, a student told me that she didn't want to meditate anymore—she just wanted to talk. So I invited her to the interview room and said, "Fine, let's talk."

She said, "I'm very happy. It's as if, in one instant, the whole world brightened up. I looked out the window, and everything was so beautiful. The birds and flowers, everything, is just part of myself. I feel very beautiful. I've gotten into it."

I asked her to tell me what she had gotten into. She said, "Isn't this what you call enlightenment?"

I told her she was just having illusions, and she became very unhappy and said, "I've made such tremendous progress, and now you tell me it's just an illusion."

I told her that it is precisely her great desire for enlightenment that creates such illusions. "Go back and continue to work hard," I said.

On another retreat, a participant did not show up for afternoon meditation. I sent a couple of people to look for him and after a long while they found him in the woods. He was extremely happy and brought back a small dried twig, which he very respectfully offered to me, saying, "I've gotten it!"

I took the twig and threw it out the window. He became upset, angry in fact, and complained that it was a precious thing that he had worked hard to get. What do you think about this precious thing?

In both of these cases the students had worked hard and achieved a deep experience. But enlightenment is not a possession you can hold on to, as if it were a jewel. Sometimes the mind experiences something that it takes to be enlightenment, but it is just the ego in a very happy state. It is not necessarily the narrow, selfish ego. The ego may even be identified with the universe as a whole or with divinity. But it is still the ego and not Buddha nature, which is the nature of emptiness. These feelings are illusory expressions of a larger sense of self gained through hard practice. To feel that everything in the universe is part of you is good, but it is not enlightenment.

The path to the realization of enlightenment is the Bodhisattva Path. At the beginning of the Bodhisattva Path, practitioners have already accepted the Buddhadharma (right view), and are ready to practice. They have an intellectual understanding that their bodies and minds are impermanent and constantly changing. Gradually they come to a deeper realization of what the Dharma teaches: that there is nothing that can truly be called the self. Upon realizing the emptiness of self in such a way that they can live free of self-centeredness, they become free of attachment and *duhkha*. This is the first stage of the Bodhisattva Path.

Bodhisattvas at the beginning of the second stage of the Bodhisattva Path are attached to the feeling or sense of liberation. When you feel that you are liberated, you are not, as I said before, because you still have the sense of a self that is liberated.

During the second stage of the path, bodhisattvas realize that the sensation of liberation is not true liberation, but they are still attached to that very understanding: that the sensation of liberation is not liberation. They are attached to their view.

At the third stage of the path, a bodhisattva is no longer attached to the self, to the sensation of liberation, to the view that the sensation of liberation is not liberation, or to anything.

If during practice you feel the rising and manifestation of wisdom, you should consider it a natural phenomenon that accompanies practice. However, when true wisdom arises it comes undetected and unannounced. Like the melting of ice under hot water, it occurs without self-consciousness on the part of the ice. The wise person has no special feeling of being wise.

Once an American who felt he had experienced enlightenment ten years earlier asked me to officially certify it. I asked him how he reacted to fame, self-interest, sex, and wealth. He said that his mind was always free and he was not attached to these things, but his body still needed them. What stage do you think he was at? First stage, of course. If he were to come to you, you wouldn't certify him, would you? But if you hadn't read this, then perhaps you would have.

There is a *gongan* about this. Master Weishan Lingyu asked two disciples, "What do you say about this? There are millions of lions, all simultaneously appearing on the tip of a hair."

Since the two disciples had been practicing, they did not think this was an outrageous idea. A strand of hair has two tips, so the first disciple, Yangshan Huizhi (approx. 807–883), replied, "A hair has two tips. On which tip do the lions appear?"

The master asked the other disciple to answer the question and he replied, "Simultaneously appearing, therefore there could be no before or after, no this end or that end."

The first disciple shook his head no, so the master asked him, "If you don't accept this, what do you have to say?"

Yangshan just stood up and walked out. The master turned to the other disciple and said, "You're finished. Your lion has been cut in half."

Does anyone here have anything to say about this?

Student: It sounds like the fellow who didn't walk out was at the second stage. He had a nice idea, a nice view, which he was representing verbally.

You're smart. He said, "No before, no after; no above, no below," but he still had a middle, the present. He had a beautiful view of the whole and he was attached to that. He was in the second stage of the Bodhisattva Path.

What stage would you say the first disciple was at? The one who asked on which tip of the hair the lions were? When he got up and walked out, what was that? Did he know the answer or not?

The master in this *gongan* was Weishan and the disciple was Yangshan. Together they formed the Wei-yang sect of Ch'an. Eventually that sect died out, but Master Xuyun, my grand master, revived its practices in the twentieth century.

Yangshan was at the third stage, when both enlightenment and the person enlightened disappear. He was no longer attached to self, sensation, view, or anything. In the Ch'an sect we advocate going straight to the third stage. If you realize sudden enlightenment, you don't need to pass through the first two stages.

What stage do you think someone is at who thinks, "I'm enlightened, and I can save sentient beings"? Third?

Student: No. Second.

Yes, this is the second level, because the practitioner is attached to a view. A bodhisattva in the first stage of the Bodhisattva Path has the feeling that he is enlightened, and he is attached to that.

When we get to the third section of the Bodhisattva Path, the highest mountain peak and the lowest valley are the same. Think of this: from the point of view of someone in a satellite looking down at the earth, the highest peak of the Himalayas is the lowest point, or closest point, and the deepest point in the ocean is the highest point. Everything is inverted from that point of view. In relationship to the whole, including both points of view, which is high and which is low?

A bodhisattva at the third level has no sense of joy or suffering, but his body feels normal sensations. For instance, if he has not eaten he will feel hunger, but he will not be greedy for food. If the weather is cold or hot, he will feel the sensation of cold or heat, but he will not feel annoyed by that. If a woman happens to touch him, he will feel that too, but it will not cause any mental vexation to arise.

A bodhisattva does not have any views. She has none of the ordinary kind of mental processes, except in order to help sentient beings. Her mental process does not include any vocabulary or any specific thoughts at all, and she has no sense of enlightenment or that her wisdom is shining outward. Out of emptiness, she naturally and spontaneously reacts to the needs of sentient beings and aids them along the Bodhisattva Path. But from the point of view of sentient beings, bodhisattvas seem enlightened and their wisdom seems to illuminate the world around them.

Before he realized enlightenment, the Ming Dynasty master Zibo read a poem by an earlier Ch'an master that said, "Cutting off vexation, vexation is increased." He was puzzled, and thought that perhaps the author or the copyist (because of course the poem was copied by hand) had made a mistake. He thought, "Doesn't cutting off vexation lead to liberation? How can cutting off vexation create more vexation?"

Now that you have heard about the third stage of the Bodhisattva Path, do you understand why the master said, "Cutting off vexation, vexation is increased"?

If you think that there is vexation to be cut off, and you want to cut off that vexation, then you are at the beginning of the Bodhisattva Path. If you think that you have cut off vexation, then at best you have completed the first section. At the third stage, you don't think of cutting off vexation or seeking wisdom because there is no such thing as vexation or wisdom. You don't need to become a Buddha because there is no such thing as a Buddha. There is no discrimination whatsoever.

The third section of the Bodhisattva Path may seem a little far off. In the beginning we still have to think in terms of vexation being cut off, and we still have to believe that there is such a thing as a Buddha we can become. Do you understand?

I vow to deliver innumerable sentient beings.

I vow to cut off endless vexations.

I vow to master limitless approaches to Dharma.

I vow to attain supreme Buddhahood.

The Bodhisattva Path, the realization of wisdom, can be seen as stages of selflessness and nonattachment, as I have just described. But enlightenment can also be seen as activity. Enlightenment means that you have come to realize what you didn't realize before. Ch'an recognizes four levels of the activity of enlightenment, and these levels unfold, one after another, over and over again.

At each level you attain a different kind of wisdom. The first level of enlightenment is to hear the Buddhadharma, which gives you the wisdom to answer some of the questions in your life. The second level is to think about the Dharma in order to better understand what you have heard. The wisdom from this level helps you answer questions about the Dharma, and about practice. The third level of enlightenment is to practice what you have learned, both formally in meditations, chanting, prostrations, etc., and in daily life. The wisdom gained from practice is deeper and allows you to better understand questions you may have about life, your self, and the Dharma. Through practice you learn more about your body, mind, and behavior. Eventually you will experience directly what you have learned intellectually. This is the fourth level of enlightenment, when you illuminate your mind and see your intrinsic nature. This is sudden enlightenment. Wisdom becomes visible because vexation and self-centeredness disappear. In that moment, all problems and questions are resolved.

Many practitioners like to focus exclusively on the fourth level of enlightenment, and they neglect the first three stages: listening, studying, and practicing in meditation and daily life. They want to bypass the preliminary activities and instantly illuminate their minds and reveal their wisdom. Such people are naive and have a poor understanding of Ch'an practice.

Even if you experience the fourth level of enlightenment, it doesn't mean that you have attained Buddhahood. In fact, the enlightenment experience may last only a moment. You will go through the four levels over and over again. Each time you will begin at a new place and learn new things. Each time you will have different experiences. By repeating this cycle again and again, eventually you can reach complete enlightenment. But we must all start at the beginning. Now you are learning about Buddhadharma. Please practice and cultivate the Dharma as well. Don't seek the fourth level. Just practice. The fourth level will manifest naturally in its own time.

7.

Compassion

Compassion was the beginning of Buddhism, and it is the essence of Buddhism. Shakyamuni Buddha practiced and manifested compassion throughout his life. We might even say that he appeared in the world to manifest compassion.

The Buddha became a practitioner because he saw the suffering of life and he wanted to know the reasons for it. He saw vexation of sentient beings and the reality of birth, old age, sickness, and death. This caused him to reflect upon his own situation: that he, too, must go through the processes of birth, old age, sickness, and death. The Buddha set out to practice not only to benefit himself, to alleviate his own suffering, but because of his concern for all sentient beings and his compassion for what seemed to be their unavoidable destiny.

At the end of Buddha's life, after forty-nine years of teaching and helping sentient beings, those who were able to be liberated during his life had been liberated, and he had planted the seeds of future liberation in those who were yet to be liberated. Thus Shakyamuni Buddha manifested compassion from the beginning through the end of his life, so compassion is the heart and essence of Buddhism. Compassion was not separate from the everyday realities of Buddha's life, and although we cannot practice compassion at the level he practiced it, it should not be separate from our lives.

Like Buddhism, most religions talk about compassion and teach loving kindness, and many people aspire to these. Nonetheless, we often limit our love to our own families or communities. When we confront other religions or spiritual practices, we give rise to animosity. Other practices are not understood, and are seen as demonic. From the perspective of the Buddhadharma, although there are differences, all sentient beings possess the potential to transform animosity and seemingly demonic and negative behavior into compassion. Therefore, from the perspective of Buddhism, there is no fixed *Mara*, or evil. Mara, like all phenomena, is empty. If Mara is able to experience and make use of the Dharma, then Mara can become compassionate. It is because everyone has the potential for compassion that compassion is the essence of Buddhism.

Although everyone has the potential for compassion, some people seem to be our enemies. How should we react to them? Shakyamuni Buddha encountered many people who wanted to harm him during his life, but he was never angry with them, nor did he try to overpower or dominate them. Instead he treated them compassionately and tried to help them. Both Buddhism in general and Ch'an in particular condemn fighting and advocate nonopposition to one's enemies. A true practitioner responds to obstructions caused by people, situations, and the environment with nonopposition, and lets go of any tension she may feel. She does not resist or fight with difficulties.

What is nonopposition? If someone treats you maliciously, do not fight with her. Instead, do everything in your power to peacefully avoid a confrontation. Even if she punches you, don't fight back. Abandon any thought of retaliation. Do not even hope that she doesn't hit you again. Such a hope is vain and unprofitable. Simply accept adversity without resistance. Do not become annoyed when faced with difficulties. To do so merely adds difficulty to difficulty and further disturbs your mind. By maintaining a mind of peace and nonopposition, difficulties will naturally fall away.

If treated with compassion, those who seem to be our enemies can take up the Dharma and become compassionate. We are all able to become compassionate because our negative nature is not fixed. It is impermanent and empty, like all phenomena. It is because of greed, hatred, and ignorance that beings manifest actions that are harmful to others.

You may wonder why we should be concerned about alleviating suffering if we believe that everything is impermanent and nothing is really good or bad. This brings up an important point in the Buddhadharma. Suffering is similar to leg pains. While you are sitting in meditation, your leg becomes painful. But as soon as you stretch out, the pain goes away. There is no question that it hurts, but the pain is not real in the sense that it is not permanent. It is capable of changing and disappearing, so it is inherently empty. The same is true of good and bad. They are subject to change. Bad can become good and good can become bad. There is an old story of a father whose son had an accident and became lame. His neighbors were sorry for him, and said that it was a tragedy. The man said, "Is that so?"

A war began and all of the young men in the village were drafted into the army. However, the lame son was not drafted, so the father's neighbors then said that he was very lucky. The man again answered, "Is that so?" What do you think?

Like good and bad, suffering exists because of the way we perceive things at a particular time and from a particular point of view. What is important is that you understand the nature of suffering. If you truly grasp that it is impermanent, and that its source is in self-centeredness, you can learn to alleviate it.

When it comes to seeing the suffering of others, reflect on your own experience. Even though you tell yourself that suffering is empty, you still experience it. Likewise, even though other people's suffering is nonexistent, you cannot deny their experience. As far as they are concerned, it is direct and real. Thus, with the understanding that suffering is unreal, you respond to that unreal experience and you strive out of compassion to alleviate the suffering of others.

How do we practice compassion and alleviate suffering? There are different levels of compassion, and the first is compassion for those who are close to us, such as our families and friends. We should want to bring happiness to these people unconditionally. "Unconditionally" means that we do not seek any reward or ask for recognition but act purely because of compassion itself. It is important to understand the difference between "compassion" in the Buddhist sense and "worldly love." The Second Noble Truth taught by the Buddha is that suffering, *duhkha*, is caused by desire, and desire is closely related to worldly love. Desire is the urge to get something. As long as we live, we have both physical and psychological desires. Physical desires are limited and can be satisfied, at least temporarily, but psychological desires are unlimited and can never be totally satisfied. Psychological desires can also intensify physical desires.

Worldly love is the urge to hold on to what we have, and attachment to things we have or desire. Ordinary people's love for someone or something is self-centered, involves desire, and seeks to possess, control, or get something from the object of love. Compassion, on the other hand, is unconditional. It is not possessive, is not self-centered, does not try to control, nor does it require recognition, reward, or love in return. Worldly love is not a bad thing. It brings harmony and kindness into human society, especially in its less self-centered forms.

As there are levels of compassion, there are also degrees or levels of worldly love, depending on the scope of the self-centeredness of the love. The most impure love is the most selfish: love of oneself. When one is only concerned with personal benefit, one exhibits this kind of love.

A young woman I know got married to an older man. She liked to go out and dance, but her husband didn't have the time or energy for such things. When he forbade her to go out, she said, "Don't you love me at all?"

He said, "Of course I love you! That is why I don't want you to go out."

The woman said, "Love means sacrificing oneself. If you love me you should sacrifice yourself for my sake."

What do you think? Who should do the sacrificing? What should they do? If the wife is concerned for her husband, she has to limit her desire to dance, and stay home. If the husband is concerned for his wife, he must limit his desire to have her at home, and let her go out. Both of them have problems. Each is concerned only with himself or herself, and wants the other to make the sacrifices.

We all know that love should motivate us to give, to be concerned for the other person. However, in situations affecting our well-being, our wealth, and our desires, how many of us can give rather than trying to take? It is possible, but it is difficult. Even within the limited scope of those close to us, whom we love, we seem incapable of being truly unselfish. It is impossible for us to forgo seeking our own benefit.

Worldly love is called "impure love" in Buddhism. Completely unselfish love is pure love, and it is the same as compassion. In the Buddhist sutras, giving, or *dana* in Sanskrit, is divided into internal giving and external giving. External giving consists of giving of your property, your time, your abilities, and so on. Internal giving consists of giving your body or even your life. It is easier to give your property, and harder to give your time and abilities, to help others. The most difficult is to give your body or your life. It is only when one is capable of giving away even one's life that one is completely free of self-centeredness.

If we have compassion, unconditional love, for those close to us, will we ourselves benefit from developing such compassion? Yes, when we put ourselves at the service of others, offering our abilities and ourselves to try to bring them lasting happiness, the process of compassionate action will cause us to be diligent in improving our abilities and will lead to spiritual maturity.

What if those we try to help are not responsive to our compassionate actions? We should not look for anything in return for our compassion. However, such people may eventually be touched by compassion and join us in the work of compassion. This is the greatest result one can produce.

For over forty years the Ch'an organization that I direct in Taiwan has been doing social welfare work. We began with an annual event to help the poor in the Pei-tou district in Taipei. We distributed food, clothing, and other things that people use every day, such as soap.

The original small social welfare group has developed into the Society for Cultivating the Field of Merit. It consists mostly of laypeople and students, and has spread beyond Taipei to all parts of Taiwan. One of the leaders of the organization recently told me that thirty years ago he was one of the people who received help from us. His family had little clothing and no food, and our organization was particularly kind to them because of their extreme poverty. We gave extra used clothing to this family, as well as food and other necessities. In gratitude, he joined the Society for Cultivating the Field of Merit and has become a leader. After hearing his story I felt very content and quite happy.

At the second level of compassion we have compassion for everyone. We have ceased to discriminate between those close to us and everyone else, and we offer service and dedicate our lives to the benefit of all sentient beings. However, although we see all sentient beings as equal at this level, there are still traces of dualism in our minds. There is still the perception of the dualism of self and others, and there is still the dualism of self and the action of compassion.

A story from Taiwan illustrates the second level of compassion. A Buddhist's wife was killed by a taxi in a hit-and-run accident. Witnesses wrote down the license plate number of the taxi, and the driver was caught by the police and prosecuted.

The judge asked the taxi driver whether he saw the woman or not. And the taxi driver replied, "Yes, I did."

The judge asked, "Why did you hit her? Was it an accident?"

The driver very honestly said, "I saw the lady but I had the right of way and she was supposed to let me pass by. When she did not, I was annoyed and I wanted to scare her by tapping her. I did not know that she was killed when I took off."

The judge decided that this was an intentional killing, so the taxi driver was sentenced to a long prison term.

The driver had a wife and children who were completely dependent on his income. When the husband of the dead woman discovered this, he helped the driver's family by taking them food, money, and whatever else they needed to survive. Beyond that, he visited the jail to see the driver, comforting him and advising him to recite Buddha's name and to practice repentance. The husband's friends were shocked and said, "How can you help the family of the man who killed your wife?"

The husband answered, "The taxi driver acted out of ignorance, but I cannot be ignorant. The heart of Buddhism is compassion, so it is natural for a Buddhist to have compassion, especially for those in need. The family was starving, so I saw it as my duty to help them."

This is an example of equality of compassion, the second level. Eventually this man left lay life to become a monk and continue his practice.

The third level of compassion is grounded on the equanimity of mind of the previous level, but there is no longer a sense of self, of other, or of compassion. The practitioner manifests compassion naturally, without any concept of self, of other people who are being helped, or of compassionate acts.

This state cannot be arrived at intentionally, nor can it be fabricated. You cannot realize the third level by telling yourself not to think about the self, others, and compassion. You must truly be in the state of selflessness, the state of wisdom. This, in Buddhism, is called the union of emptiness and compassion. Self, others, and events, indeed all dualities, are dissolved and empty, and yet the activity of compassion functions. This is the compassion of buddhas and great bodhisattvas.

The *Diamond Sutra* says, ". . . deliver innumerable sentient beings inexhaustibly, yet not one sentient being is delivered." This expresses thorough emptiness and compassion. Only buddhas and great practitioners are able to do this. The Buddha delivered sentient beings without conceiving that he was a buddha who was helping sentient beings, and without conceiving of the action of helping.

I cannot give you an exact example of this, but I can tell you a story that approximates it. In the Sung Dynasty (960–1279), there was an eccentric Ch'an master called Jigong, whose formal name was Daoji. He was famous in the city where he lived, and even in distant parts of China. His biography has not been translated into English, but Tibetans know about him and equate him with the eccentric Tibetan Buddhist master Milarepa.

Unlike most *bhiksus*, Master Jigong never lived in a monastery nor had any other fixed place of abode. Instead, he roamed around the city. In winter he wore a thin, ragged robe, similar in style to the one I wear, but he didn't have a shirt or pants or underwear to wear under his robe, or socks or shoes, or a hat for winter. However, he was quite happy. There was an official in the city who admired him and became his devotee. One winter day Master Jigong passed the residence of this official, who, upon seeing him dressed in a rag with nothing underneath, asked, "Master, it is cold out. Shouldn't you put on more clothing?"

Jigong said, "Yes, yes, I should."

"Why don't you put on a hat? At least wear pants and a shirt under your robe and put on some shoes," said the official.

"Yes, yes, I should," Jigong responded.

"So, why don't you?" asked the official.

"I don't have anything to put on," said Jigong.

The official took pity on Jigong and said, "I will give you cloth to make clothing so you can live through the winter. How much fabric do you need?"

Jigong said, "Well, I need quite a lot. I would like to have two hats so that I can change and alternate on different days. I need to have shirts and pants to wear under my robe, and, of course, underwear. Fine cotton would be better than ordinary fabric and it should be double-padded so it is really warm. I need fabric for my shoes. So I need quite a lot."

The official gave Jigong a whole roll of cotton fabric.

Jigong looked at the roll of fabric and said, "What am I going to do with this? I don't have money to pay to have clothes made, and I myself don't know how to sew. I think I need some money, too. Lots of it."

The official said, "I will give you another roll of fabric and you can exchange it for sewing."

Jigong left the official's house lugging two heavy rolls of fabric. He got to a bridge where beggars congregated. Seeing him, they said, "Jigong, what have you got there? What do you need all that fabric for? All of us need clothes. Give some to us."

Jigong smiled and said, "Sure, take what you need."

The gang of beggars quickly split the fabric up and Jigong was left with nothing. He walked away happily in his ragged robe, still with no underwear, no pants, no shoes, no hats, and no shirts.

Sometime later the official saw that Jigong was still wearing nothing but his ragged robe. The official asked, "What happened to your new clothes?"

Jigong said, "What new clothes?"

"The ones you had made from the fabric I gave you."

"Oh, the fabric. The fabric was given to the beggars," said Jigong. "They had nothing to wear and were very pitiable. Worse than me. So I need some more fabric. Do you have any?"

The official said, "I will give you more, but this time you have to make clothing for yourself," and he gave Jigong two more rolls of fabric.

Jigong once again set out lugging two rolls of fabric. This time, before he even reached the bridge all the beggars in town heard the news that he had more fabric and came running to beg for it. Again, Jigong happily gave it all away.

Jigong dared not pass by the official's residence anymore. When the official heard the news that the mad monk had been giving away fabric again, he thought to himself, "Jigong is really something. I gave him four rolls of fabric and he did not keep any for himself, but gave them all away. He is indeed a fool. Therefore, I won't try to help him anymore. This door of charity will be closed to him from now on."

Ch'an Master Jigong was, in fact, a realized practitioner and completely selfless. Whatever he had, he gave for the benefit of those around him, without any sense of loss, gain, or reward. He simply remained happy. Master Jigong's actions and mind were free from self-attachment. After giving away everything, his mind was as if nothing had happened: no trace whatsoever remained of giving or of helping anyone. His actions were, in the true sense, compassionate.

The official in the story was different. His charitable deeds were governed by many conditions. He only wished to give away fabric to Ch'an Master Jigong, the person he respected, and not to the beggars. When his perspective on Jigong changed, and he decided that Jigong was not a person worthy of respect, but a fool, the official stopped being sympathetic, kind, and charitable. What he gave was limited. For most of us, our compassion or sympathy is very much conditioned. When we find ourselves in similar situations, most of us behave like the official. It is very difficult to give help without prerequisites, conditions, and limits. Unconditional compassion, the mind to benefit others, is not something easy to realize.

Compassion always exists together with wisdom. True compassion can only arise out of wisdom, out of selflessness. The third type of compassion arises out of great, unconditional wisdom. We can also call this great love. It is love that is no longer tainted by self-attachment, vexation, gaining, losing, or any kind of self-interest. It is the Buddha's wisdom, which manifests as the pure heart of compassion.

There was a Dharma master who was charitable, compassionate, kind, and loving. He was very helpful to other people. I know this because he told me so. He would also say, "Such and such a person is doing well today because I helped him at such and such a time in the past. I have helped so many people, yet they all are like people who destroy the bridge after they have crossed it. They never mention my help. Now that they are successful, they do not even remember me. I myself do not mind this. In fact, I have forgotten about all of them and I still continue to help people."

This master did indeed help many people, and he did not ask for any reward from those he helped. However, there were traces of these events in his mind. As a matter of fact, they left such an imprint on his mind that they were often on his lips. Do you recognize these kinds of traces in yourself? What level of compassion was this man manifesting, do you think?

When most people begin practice, their goal is to become liberated, to be enlightened, and to be free from suffering, but they are unconcerned about compassion. Do you think they are able to realize wisdom? To become enlightened?

Buddhist compassion and wisdom are always found together. They are like the two wings of a bird, working in harmony so that the bird can soar through the vastness of the sky. Without the wing of wisdom, compassion will not be genuine, selfless compassion. Compassion is always guided by the insight of wisdom. Without it there can only be sympathy, worldly love, or ordinary kindness, all of which are conditional, governed by an objective, and tainted with attachment, mental defilement, and self-centered emotions.

Is it possible to have wisdom without compassion? No. Without the wing of compassion, wisdom cannot arise. A person without compassion is selfish, and that is not wisdom.

All the diverse practices of the Dharma help us develop compassion. The same practices lead us toward wisdom. For example, the purpose of practicing the six *paramitas*—giving, upholding the precepts, patience/endurance, diligence, concentration/*samadhi*, and wisdom—is to benefit sentient beings. We give our money, time, energy, and whatever else we have for the benefit of sentient beings. We uphold precepts and refrain from doing harm through body, speech, and mind, restrain our desires and purify ourselves, all for the purpose of benefiting sentient beings. We endure whatever happens to us, and cultivate patience and diligence in order to deliver sentient beings.

People may think that the fifth *paramita*, the cultivation of concentration or *samadhi*, has nothing to do with benefiting others. After all, one engages in *samadhi* practice by oneself, sitting in meditation, chanting, prostrating, or walking. However, *samadhi* practice is also for the purpose of benefiting sentient beings. Shakyamuni Buddha perfected all levels of *samadhi* in order to find ways to help sentient beings. Therefore, for all of us practitioners, the practice of concentration, the practice of mental cultivation, is for the purpose of mastering our minds so that we let go of self-centeredness and become more capable of helping others.

All the *paramitas* arise from compassion and the desire to bring lasting happiness to sentient beings. In the process of benefiting others, we ourselves are benefited. This is a very crucial point. We are not really separate, and all of our welfare is intertwined. You can see this in a mundane way when you cause yourself suffering. When we ourselves experience *duhkha*, such as anger, we often influence others and cause them *duhkha* as well. If we are compassionate toward ourselves and do not cause ourselves *duhkha*, we will not cause it in others, either. If we engage in the diverse practices of the Dharma, eventually the wisdom of selflessness manifests and we become compassionate. As we progress, the perfection of wisdom comes about through compassion. So find your wings of wisdom and compassion, and realize the extinction of suffering!

Glossary

A

AMITABHA BUDDHA: The Buddha of the Western Paradise of the Pure Land sect. (*See* "Pure Land.")

ANATMAN: *See* "Three marks."

ARHAT: "Worthy one." In Buddhist tradition, the arhat is thought of as having completed the course of Buddhist practice, and has attained liberation, or nirvana. As such, the arhat is no longer subject to rebirth and death. Arhat is also one of the epithets of the Buddha.

AVALOKITESVARA: Perhaps the most important bodhisattva in the Chinese Buddhist tradition; he is the embodiment of compassion who hears and responds to the cries of all living beings.

Avalokitesvara can be both male or female, but in China the bodhisattva is usually depicted in the female form.

B

BHIKSU, BHIKSUNI: Fully ordained Buddhist monk and nun, respectively.

BODHI: Can refer to: the principal wisdom that severs all vexations and defilements, and realizes nirvana; or, the wisdom that realizes that every conditioned phenomenon can realize omniscience.

BODHIDHARMA: The twenty-eighth patriarch after Shakyamuni Buddha in the Indian lineage, and the first Chinese patriarch of Ch'an.

BODHI-MIND: The mind of wisdom. A central idea in Mahayana Buddhism; its meaning varies in different contexts: 1) the altruistic mind of a person who aspires to attain Buddhahood for the sake of helping sentient beings; 2) the genuine actualization of enlightenment, awakening to the true nature of reality and the loftiness of Buddhahood; and 3) selfless action. This last meaning is extremely important yet often overlooked. Arousing the bodhi-mind is the first step in establishing oneself on the Bodhisattva Path.

BODHISATTVA: "Enlightened being." The role model in the Mahayana tradition. The bodhisattva is a being who vows to remain in the world of *samsara*, postponing his/her own full liberation until all other living beings are delivered.

BODHISATTVA PATH: The way to bodhisattvahood begins with arousing the thought of enlightenment and the goal of cultivating merit and virtue for the sake of sentient beings.

BODHI TREE: The fig tree under which the historical Buddha attained Complete Enlightenment.

BUDDHA: "The awakened one." The historical Buddha is the religious teacher Gautama Shakyamuni, who founded the religion generally known in the West as "Buddhism."

BUDDHADHARMA: The truths and the teaching of Buddhism; the Dharma as taught by the Buddha. (*See* "Dharma.")

BUDDHAHOOD: Realization of Supreme Enlightenment.

BUDDHA-NATURE: The nature or potentiality of Buddhahood; synonym for the nature of emptiness. It is also equivalent to *tathagatagarbha*.

BUDDHISM: Founded by the historical Buddha, Shakyamuni, in the sixth century B.C. The basic thought of Buddhism is summed up in the Tripitaka. The Buddhist community consists of monks and nuns as well as lay followers.

C

CAUSE AND CONSEQUENCE: Cause and effect according to the law of karma.

CH'AN: Better known in Japanese as "Zen." Ch'an is one of the main schools of Chinese Buddhism to develop during the T'ang Dynasty (618–907). The designation derives from the Sanskrit *dhyana*, transliterated as *chan-na* in Chinese. *Ch'an* can mean "meditation," but it can also mean the heart of Buddhism—enlightenment.

COMPASSION: One of the two essential aspects of enlightenment; the other is wisdom.

D

DHARMA: Dharma has two basic meanings. Dharma with an uppercase *D* means the Buddhist "law" or "teaching." Dharma with a lowercase *d* simply refers to a thing, a feeling, time, weather, etc.: any physical or mental phenomenon.

DHARMADHATU: Dharma-realm, the infinite realms or worlds of reality; it can also be regarded as the ground or nature of all things—the Mind from which all proceeds.

DHARMAKAYA: Dharma-body. One of the three bodies of the Buddha—the ultimate body of reality beyond all forms, attributes, and limits. In the Chinese Buddhist tradition, the expression "to see the Dharmakaya" means to realize the nature of emptiness. It is sometimes used as a synonym for Buddha-nature.

DHYANA: A term designating certain states of meditative absorption cultivated by Buddhist practitioners as a technique for attaining enlightenment. However, *dhyana* can also refer to a practice after enlightenment, in which one cultivates solely the nondual quiescent and still nature of mind.

DIAMOND SUTRA: Sanskrit: *Vajracchedika Sutra*. A sutra belonging to the Prajnaparamita (Perfection of Wisdom) system of literature, which expounds on the ultimate truth of emptiness. With the *Heart Sutra,* it is one of the most important scriptures in the Ch'an (and Zen) schools.

DUHKHA: Often translated from Sanskrit as "suffering," *duhkha* includes the ideas that life is impermanent and that it is often experienced as unsatisfactory.

E

ENLIGHTENMENT: Self-realization.

F

FOUR NOBLE TRUTHS: The four basic principles of Buddhism preached by Buddha in his first sermon: 1) in the ultimate analysis, life is suffering; 2) the cause of suffering is desire; 3) there is a state of peace called nirvana, beyond all suffering and poisons of the mind; and 4) the way that leads to nirvana includes the practice of morality, concentration, and wisdom.

G

GONGAN: Japanese: *koan.* A "public case," as in a law case. A Ch'an method of meditation in which the practitioner energetically and single-mindedly pursues the answer to an enigmatic question either posed by the master or arising spontaneously. The question can be answered only by abandoning logic and reasoning, through directly generating and breaking through the "doubt sensation" under natural causes and conditions. Famous *gongan* encounters were recorded and used by masters to test their disciples' understanding, or they served as catalysts for enlightenment. The term *gongan* is often used interchangeably with *hua to*.

H

HINAYANA: The "lesser vehicle" of those who strive mainly for their own personal liberation from suffering by destroying greed, hatred, and delusion. In contrast, Mahayana, or the "great vehicle," is the broader teaching of the bodhisattva who, out of compassion, puts his/her own salvation last and uses all available means to save sentient beings.

HUA TO: "The source of words" (before they are uttered), a method used in the Ch'an school to arouse the "doubt sensation." The practitioner meditates on such baffling questions as: "What is nothingness?," "Where am I?," or "Who is reciting the Buddha's name?" One does not rely on experience, logic, or reasoning. Often, these phrases are taken from *gongans*; at other times, they are spontaneously generated by the practitioner. The term *hua to* is often used interchangeably with the Japanese *koan*.

I

IMPERMANENCE: *See* "Three marks."
INVESTIGATION: Asking or querying in order to penetrate the meaning of a *hua to*.

K

KARMA: "Action." Basically, the law of cause and effect to which all sentient beings—indeed, all things—are subject. Karma is broadly construed in Buddhism to include physical, verbal, and mental actions. It is also the cumulative causal situation affecting one's destiny as a result of past acts, thoughts, emotions.

KARMIC AFFINITY: A bond or connection between people due to a relationship (either good or bad) formed in a previous life. Frequently such an affinity is discussed in terms of "causes and conditions." "Cause" focuses on the specific karmic disposition of the individual; "conditions" refer to the nexus of causes that make up his situation.

KARMIC ROOTS: The (mental) disposition of sentient beings due to their past karma. For example, people who learn quickly and can easily generate faith, who can take up the practice of the Dharma and derive beneficial results directly, are said to have "good karmic roots." This is due to their previous cultivation of and affinity for the Dharma.

KARMIC SEEDS: Actions that will result in consequences in the future.

L

LIBERATION: Liberation from the illusions that cause self-centeredness and suffering.

LIN-CHI SCHOOL: Japanese: *Rinzai*. One of two existing Ch'an lineages.

LINEAGE: Line of masters in Ch'an, Zen, and some other forms of Buddhism. When a teacher recognizes that a student has a sufficient level of spiritual insight, he or she acknowledges that ceremonially and the student becomes part of the teacher's lineage.

LOTUS SUTRA: Sanskrit: *Saddharmapundarika Sutra*. "The Sutra of the Lotus of the True Dharma." One of the earliest and most influential scriptures in the Mahayana, translated six times into Chinese between 255–601 A.D. The *Lotus Sutra* describes the bodhisattva ideal, and holds that the perfect vehicle to ultimate liberation is the Great Vehicle, the Mahayana.

LOVING KINDNESS: The altruistic aspiration for the welfare of other beings. Compassion.

M

MAHAYANA: "Great Vehicle," whose followers vow to attain Supreme Enlightenment for the sake of delivering all other sentient beings from suffering.

MARA: "Murder" or "destruction" in Sanskrit. Mara is also the name of the lord of the sixth desire realm in Buddhist mythol-

ogy, who tried to prevent Shakyamuni from realizing enlightenment by tempting and threatening him.

MIDDLE WAY: Avoidance of all extremes.

N

NIRVANA: Total extinction of desire and suffering; the state of
liberation through full enlightenment.

P

PATRIARCH: Great master or founder of a school, and his
successors in the transmission of its teaching.

PLATFORM SUTRA: A scripture attributed to the seventh-
century Ch'an master, Huineng (638–713), who was the Sixth
Patriarch in the Ch'an school, and perhaps the most famous of
the Chinese patriarchs. He was the founder of the southern
school of Ch'an, which emphasized sudden enlightenment.

PRACTICE: Includes the three major endeavors of keeping the
precepts, practicing *samadhi*, and acquiring wisdom.

PRAJNA: An intuitive wisdom that cannot be conveyed by concepts or in intellectual terms. The realization of *prajna* is the
attainment of Buddhahood.

PRECEPTS: Common moral principles shared by all members
of the Sangha.

PURE LAND: Sanskrit: *Sukhavati*. The land of Supreme Bliss,
or the Western Paradise of Amitabha Buddha. It is a pure realm
perfected by the power of Amitabha Buddha's vow to save living

beings. Through Amitabha's grace, any person who sincerely invokes his name and expresses the wish to be born there will be reborn in the Pure Land. (*See* "Amitabha Buddha.")

R

REFUGE: Taking "refuge" in the Three Jewels—Buddha, Dharma, and Sangha—confirms one as a Buddhist practitioner.

RINZAI: Here, Rinzai refers to the Japanese sect of Zen derived from the Lin-chi sect of Ch'an. Lin-chi and T'sao-tung (which became Soto in Japan) are the two sects of Ch'an that have survived up to the present day.

S

SAMADHI: Like *dhyana, samadhi* also refers to states of meditative absorption, but it is a broader and more generic term than *dhyana*. Although numerous specific samadhis are mentioned in Buddhist scriptures, the term *samadhi* itself is flexible and not as specific as *dhyana*. In Mahayana sutras, "samadhi" is inseparable from "wisdom."

SAMSARA: The relentless cycle of birth and death and suffering, in which ordinary, unenlightened sentient beings are deeply entangled. There are three realms within *samsara*: desire, form, and the formless.

SANGHA: The Buddhist community; originally Shakyamuni Buddha's immediate disciples. In a limited sense it consists of Buddhist monks, nuns, and disciples; in a broader sense it includes all persons connected through belief in and practice of Buddhism.

SASTRAS: One of the "three baskets" of the Tripitaka. Sastra is a book of treatise, discourse, discussion, and commentary clarifying, or sometimes systematizing, Buddhist philosophical ideas from the sutras.

SENTIENT BEINGS: All beings that experience pain and suffering; differentiated from nonsentient beings like plants, which do not experience pain and suffering.

SHAKYAMUNI BUDDHA: The historical Buddha who lived in northern India during the sixth century, B.C. Son of a provincial king, he renounced the royal life, practiced austerities in the forest for six years, and finally attained Supreme Enlightenment. The rest of his life was spent wandering and teaching, thereby laying the foundations of Buddhism.

SHIKANTAZA: Literally, "just mind sitting." A form of Ch'an and Zen meditation practice.

SILENT ILLUMINATION (*MO CHAO*): The method of using no method. "Silent" means no thoughts; the mind is not moving. "Illumination" means that the mind is clear, and that awareness is pure consciousness.

SIX PARAMITAS: "Six perfections" or ways for transcending to liberation. The six *paramitas* are the main practices of Mahayana bodhisattvas: giving, morality, patience, diligence, meditation, and wisdom.

SOTO: *See* "Rinzai."

SURANGAMA SUTRA: This Mahayana sutra is extremely important in shaping the uniqueness of Chinese Buddhism. It describes twenty-five different perfect penetration *samadhis* to reach thorough enlightenment, the positive and negative experiences a practitioner may encounter, and fifty different outer-path practices that one can stray into.

SUTRAS: Generally, scriptures. Specifically, the recorded "open" teachings of the Buddha that can be practiced by anyone. The distinctive mark of a Buddhist sutra is the opening line, "Thus have I heard." This indicates that what follows are the direct teachings of Buddha, as remembered and recorded by his disciples.

T

TATHAGATA: One of the ten epithets of a Buddha, which can mean "thus-come" or "thus-gone." The Chinese translation of Tathagata means "thus-come."

TATHAGATAGARBHA: Womb, or store, of the Tathagata—the potentiality of Buddhahood in each sentient being. Another name for Buddha-nature.

THREE KINDS OF ACTIONS/KARMA: Physical actions, speech, and thought.

THREE MARKS: The three marks of everything existing: *anitya*, impermanence; *duhkha*, suffering; *anatman*, nonessentiality.

TRANSFORMATION BODY: Nirmanakaya. One of the three bodies of the Buddha, the form that a Buddha manifests to facilitate the deliverance of sentient beings.

TRANSMISSION: From heart-mind to heart-mind, "receiving" the Buddhadharma from one's master.

TSAO-TUNG SCHOOL: Japanese: *soto*. One of two existing Ch'an lineages.

V

VEXATION: The innate mechanism of possession and action, tainted by an attachment to self, which in turn continues the cycle of *samsara*. Vexations include all kinds of mental states such as joy and resentment, sadness and happiness, as well as greed, hatred, delusion, arrogance, and doubt.

W

WISDOM: One of the two essential aspects of enlightenment; the other is compassion.

Acknowledgments

The Ch'an Center runs on the dedication of the resident sangha and the energy and enthusiasm of volunteers. Like everything else that happens here, this book would not have been possible without the help of many people, including the monks and nuns, and volunteers who cook, work in the office, keep the computers running, answer phones, and so on. For help on this particular project, the Ch'an Center would especially like to thank Guo-gu Shi, who checked to make sure there were no mistakes concerning Buddhist beliefs and history; Ming-yee Wang, who did much of the translation; Giora Carmi, Simeon Gallu, Guo-huan, Ernie Heav, Trish Ing, Stuart Lachs, Robert Lapides, Chris Marano, Harry Miller, Bruce Rickenbacher, Dorothy Weiner; and all the people who helped select material for this book at the beginning of the process. We would also like to thank the people who kindly read early versions of this text: Kevin Byrne, Murray Heller, and Michelle Spark.